T0123383

DECODING THE BEAST

GRAEME TORCKLER

WESTBOW
PRESS®
A DIVISION OF THOMAS NELSON
& ZONDERVAN

Illustrations by Graeme Torckler
First Published 2014
Second Revision 2015

www.decodingthebeast.com
Direct all book inquiries to Graeme Torckler, book@decodingthebeast.com

WestBow Press books may be ordered through booksellers or by contacting:

WestBow Press
A Division of Thomas Nelson & Zondervan
1663 Liberty Drive
Bloomington, IN 47403
www.westbowpress.com
1 (866) 928-1240

ISBN: 978-1-5127-4682-2 (sc)
ISBN: 978-1-5127-4683-9 (hc)
ISBN: 978-1-5127-4681-5 (e)

Library of Congress Control Number: 2016910116

Print information available on the last page.

WestBow Press rev. date: 07/20/2016

A new-generation concept book revealed by the number 666. Thrilling revelation of hidden conspiracies interwoven throughout generations from the beginning of time.

CONTENTS

Prelude

I started writing this book in early 2011 from material I compiled over many years. As I researched and wrote this book, I watched the fulfillment of what I wrote. Now, chapter 13 of Revelation is being fulfilled before our eyes. As it's coming to pass, it's increasing in significance.

The seed germinates before the tree grows, but I think we're past even the sapling stage. As this thing heats up, we're seeing superpowers contend for world control; some are joining to become greater while others have had their day and are transforming into different entities.

I believe the year 2014 marks a most significant time in our history. Just as we have seen the Arab spring, we are seeing a Beast spring. Three important systems to help its operation are covert tracking and data collection, dictating the terms to religious entities, and mobile computing.

The year 2014 marks the year the National Security Agency (NSA) came out of the closet. Unwillingly, it was forced to begin changing its tack with the public. The agency was cloaked in secrecy and had the freedom to pursue subversive attacks on privacy and harvest all kinds of data. For over seven years, it operated with little to no public attention. Then halfway through 2013, a Judas operator fell prey to the conscious choice of human integrity and started leaking documents exposing its covert operations. Consequently, a dumbing down of NSA's intentions is in operation through its media arms while enforcement potentially increases, but we'll never be certain of the full scope of its abilities. Keep a watch on the Snowden, Dotcom, and Assange stories.

I believe that 2014 marks the beginning to the end of the Christian churches' legal freedom to operate as a morals-based church entity we've enjoyed and assumed with the full rights of tax freedom. Church groups need to have the right to say yes and no to moral issues. The tax freedoms that were freely given could now come at a moral cost. As they begin to remove the church's principal foundations, its autonomy breaks down.

Though the end of this process could be years away, we're seeing its beginning in 2014. Pastors are being legally intimidated for their preaching and forced to comply with altered marriage laws. The Christian Church has moral foundations; to remove these erodes the freedom of choices made by its members. This is most likely the beginning of commercially controlled religion; Satan is gaining momentum.

In 2014, the iPhone, the flagship of the handheld computing revolution, reached its seventh year after having become a social necessity for everyone. Even children under age seven receive tablets for Christmas, which schools are increasingly insisting they have. These children are involved in social media, mapping and tracking, commerce, education, and every type of communication with such tablets.

These three are like firestorms, forces of change that are pioneering a radical reengineering of social behavior, world opinion, and trading platforms. Prophetic words documented 1,900 years ago are being fulfilled; Revelation 13 tells us, "The time would come, whereby they could not trade without the mark." Covert tracking and data collection dictate the terms of religion; these systems are impinging on our freedom.

I'm not suggesting this is a quick-growing tree; I'm not even sure this is the generation that will witness a mature 666 system. I think this modus operandi has been with us for many centuries. From the beginning, this beastly resistance to human freedom has been developing.

This book reveals the Beast's dwelling place, what it looks like, and how it is influencing us. This will help us realize its existence and track its growth so we can say, "Right back at you, boy!" That could be scary if you allow it. Don't stir up a wild dog while it sleeps; just quietly walk around it. You'll be okay.

PART 1

CHAPTER ONE

DANIEL AND THE MAGNIFICENT FOUR

As a child, Daniel was stolen from his homeland during a brutal assault by the Babylonians led by King Nebuchadnezzar. As a well-educated young man, he was trained in a ministerial office with many other young Jews to learn the language and customs of the Chaldeans.

Daniel was selected with three others to serve the king because their knowledge, understanding, and wisdom were ten times more than that of their compatriots. He rose to prominence with Nebuchadnezzar after interpreting the king's dream. Daniel continued to increase in status while serving four kings and three kingdoms. Through all his suffering and disenfranchisement, with no nation and no human rights, Daniel never gave up hope of seeing his homeland.

Daniel's thirst for Jerusalem grew over the years, but his destiny couldn't be changed. He was owned by the kingdom he served; he had no escape. He prayed and read the Scriptures and had dreams and visions. In which he saw, terrible beasts arose from the sea and threatened the world; maybe these terrifying images evoked more feelings of hopelessness in Daniel. He saw a lion with eagle's wings, a devouring bear, a leopard with four wings, and a dreadful one, trampling and devouring the earth with iron teeth.

Daniel related well to the terror of wild beasts because he survived close encounters locked inside a den of hungry lions. This happened because his prayerful attitude had evoked jealousy among the king's traditional confidants, astrologers, and wise men determined to end Daniel's promotions. But their entrapment of Daniel was their own undoing. Daniel faced these overpowering beasts and wasn't eaten. The king, who was fond of Daniel, substituted his accusers for Daniel as the lions' meal.

Always the servant to the king and with no way out except up, Daniel was careful, loyal, and beyond reproach. But he was also burdened by his reputation as an interpreter of dreams; he understood beastly dominions. God had saved him from the lions' den, and he most certainly didn't want to go back there. Maybe the dreams caused these concerns because he perceived entrapment, death, destruction, and more hopelessness. But he also knew his God and sought the understanding as to their applications.

In the fullness of the interpretations Daniel received, these four were the chief kingdoms. They spanned periods longer than a human life. Their time lines were ratified in prophecy of seventy weeks, as was recorded in the book of Daniel, the only book in the Bible originally written mostly in Arabic rather than Hebrew.

The four beasts were described as having flesh-eating power because they used human death and the destruction of family and society as their principal weapons of control. History tells the story of their battles and their merciless killing of innocents to further their kingdoms. These allegorical entities were described in this manner.

1. **A lion with eagle's wings.** "I watched till its wings were plucked off; and it was lifted up from the earth and made to stand on two feet like a man, and a man's heart was given to it."
2. **A bear.** It was raised up on one side, and had three ribs in its mouth between its teeth. And they said thus to it, "Arise, devour much flesh!"
3. **A leopard**, which had on its back four wings of a bird. The Beast also had four heads, and dominion was given to it.
4. **A fourth beast**, dreadful, terrible, exceedingly strong. It had huge iron teeth. It was devouring, breaking in pieces, and trampling the residue with its feet and "shall devour the whole earth, trample it and break it in pieces." This fourth needs repeating as it was most terrible in comparison to the other three. "Dreadful, terrible, exceedingly strong … devour the whole earth, trample it and break it in pieces."

The four beasts were four great kingdoms that ruled or were destined to rule. Their time span was so great they continued into the Book of Revelation as written by the apostle John five to six hundred years later.

Significant kings led these dominant empires. The first was King Nebuchadnezzar of Babylon. Next came King Darius of Media-Persia. Long after Daniel passed came Alexander the Great of the Greek Empire. All had various influences over Israel and were center stage in global affairs.

Then came a very fearful dominion. Beginning with the great conquests of Julius Caesar, the great legend of the Roman Empire and the legacy of Caesar began. It continued to plunder the earth and take a strong hold in Israel during Caesar Augustus's reign. From Rome, they dominated the known world.

Daniel's dream was disturbing. He had no human answer, so he prayed for an interpretation. An angel explained the dream's meaning, which was written in the book of Daniel. The angel revealed that the dream concerned dominions and their successors throughout their periods. First, there was Babylon as a lion with four wings. Second was Media-Persia as a bear with three ribs in its mouth. The third was Greece, the leopard with four wings. Finally was Rome, the terrifying beast with iron teeth.

These kingdoms were great in their day and sequential in dominion. Rome was the last to rule, as seen in Daniel's dream. Its iron teeth deteriorated; it became a humane movement as its military power changed to a social order. Christian ethics slowly consumed the harsh dictatorship, and Constantine arose as the first Christian Roman ruler.

Daniel's visions saw further than just Rome's rule. They possibly showed the time to the beginning of the end of the world. Here is where Daniel's vision overlapped with that of the apostle John in Revelation. John lived in the days of the iron-toothed monster, the Roman Empire, and was incarcerated on the Isle of Patmos by one of the horns.

John saw and wrote about a vision described in Daniel 7:12 that the lion, bear, and leopard would remain for a time. John described how these three would look.

> Then I stood on the sand of the sea. And I saw a beast rising up out of the sea, having seven heads and ten horns, and on his horns ten crowns, and on his heads a

blasphemous name. Now the beast which I saw was like a leopard, his feet were like the feet of a bear, and his mouth like the mouth of a lion. The dragon gave him his power, his throne, and great authority. (Revelation 13:1–2 NKJV)

John saw one Beast made up of the three. Its body was that of a leopard, its feet were the feet of a bear, and its mouth was that of a lion. The fourth, the personification of Satan himself, a dragon, gave the Beast its power, throne, and authority.

This newly formed flesh-eater combined the attributes of the old empires into one global enforcer no longer focused just on Israel but on world dominion. This new version was after the new lineage of the Christian saints. Revelation 13:7 NKJV reads, "It was granted to him to make war with the saints and to overcome them. And authority was given him over every tribe, tongue, and nation."

This begins to unfold a relationship between the book of Daniel and Revelation; where Daniel ends, Revelation begins. Written some five hundred years later, John picked up with the three beasts that remained and revealed their new morphed condition—no longer three but one—and a fourth dark and sinister power controlling them.

I later reveal how these four calculate to 666 and how that number is a clue to knowing where worldwide dominion operates. We can understand that "four entities" as a primitive term in the voice in which Scripture was written. Four is a number of global governments because it is the number of the corners of the earth, the winds of the earth, and compass directions of the earth. Four is also the number of corners in the foundation of most buildings. The number of feet of each beast is also four.

Daniel's four beasts were forged from the legacies of the nations and opposed everything that stood in their way. These four entities became a collective, a single world power not in a physical body as such but in an unseen dimension. So for the purpose of this book, I try to convey how these beasts existed. Though ethereal in part, evidence suggests their existence and influence in the world was very real.

Counting Unseen Evils

Decoding the Beast relies on a cypher, a simple mathematical code found in the authorized English translation of the Bible. Counting the code of the Beast reveals the final kingdoms of the earth. The Beast of Revelation comprises multiple entities, so it could be multilateral in nature.

Hundreds of multilateral and bilateral organizations have arisen in the last ten years, and these could be the final kingdoms on earth. These countries are signing agreements with umbrella organizations that fulfill some of the concepts in Revelation.

This is not a new style of government; Caesar also created a confederation of nations through contractual agreements. Two thousand years later, a multiplicity of organizations that create and control similar contractual agreements have risen to power. Is this becoming the new global confederation of nations? "These are of one mind, and they will give their power and authority to the beast" (Revelation 17:13 NKJV).

Babylon, Media-Persia, and Greece became a confederated organization under Rome. Two thousand years later, we see organizations joining sovereign nations together.

Is This the End Time?

For the most part, end-time allusions, ideas, and predictions have created more fear than faith, more dread than clarity, and more blockbuster movies and books than conversions. I hope my concepts of what I have seen in the Bible will switch the light on and allow others to discover the Bible's relevance to our modern world.

Not all is evil. The world is run by ordinary people wanting to achieve extraordinary results sometimes for themselves and other times unselfishly for others. The human gene pool is all about living for self or for others; the struggle of right and wrong tests every person equally.

The rich and the poor come under the same scrutiny, but obligations fall more heavily on the rich, who are obligated to produce more for others or be judged accordingly. The poor will also be judged but not as harshly as the selfish rich will be. Who is the judge? Aren't we all? Do not the attitudes, opinions, and actions of us all judge us all?

So whether we're judging our current political and economic landscapes, enjoying them, of suffering under them, we're all somehow entangled by their various levels of contracts, demands, and opinions. I don't mean to point fingers or to warn only some because we're all involved with each other in some way or another whether for good or evil; it's very difficult to remove ourselves from the equation.

Rather, I want to show that the Bible warns us; its marvelous predictions are coming to light before our eyes. Even a simple calculator can reveal the wonders of these prophecies.

Power behind the Throne

Ordinary people lead our world with extraordinary authority. Unlike some end-time books, *Decoding the Beast* is not so much about gob-stopping brutality and corruption but about global control, and it offers insight into the power behind the throne. Who is in charge, and who is essentially running this planet we all love? An intelligence officer once told me that the real rulers are never obvious, that we need to look further than just the front-page news. Those chosen to front a public office are often controlled by other people, the real power behind the throne.

In the last 200 years, we have seen a shift from monarchical rule to democratic governance in religions, corporations, and organizations led by normal people sometimes chosen for their cause and sometimes through their strong personal desire to seek position and authority. Credibility to the rich is like a drug; who knows what an addict would do?

Who holds absolute power and is responsible for the rise and fall of nations? Where does our modern social engineering come from? Who is resisting the integrity of the faith? Where do the counter-information movements come from? Why would anything but the truth be considered viable?

We think we're all safe. We trust governments and their intelligently designed systems to protect us, provide for our well-being, and keep us warm at night. And for the most, these incredible political systems are working very well—over 20 percent of the world's people enjoy democratic freedom. Although now there is a power vacuum; maybe it's the other 80 percent that is beginning to swallow up many countries who want what Western nations have.

This modern, financially controlled democratic system is the best we could have developed; it exceeds by far any system of the past. Maybe this is the ultimate political system. It is a brilliant, self-correcting commercial system that controls everything. Will this financial system fall apart due to corruption and overspending? There is no real evidence so far of that; its partial collapses due to stock market and institutional failures cause recalibrations and corrections but not total failure.

The consumer aspect of our financial global empire is its only nagging drawback; the human belly is never full. Our debts with the planet are becoming greater than our debts with the bankers of the earth. Is there no way out of this? The lenders need to continue lending and the wheels of commerce need to keep turning; that is where governments control the system. When times change and things get difficult, they simply vary the system's rules so it continues to accommodate us as if nothing were wrong. It becomes just another step forward for humanity. But unlike commerce, the laws of our environment can't be so easily changed.

Our debts are our liabilities; we are all servants to our lenders, and through debt, the world is controlled. Our global economy is subject to the Golden Rule: those with the gold make the rules. They also change them when they want. But I fear our looming debts to the environment won't go away.

I'm not convinced the powers behind the thrones of commerce and government have much regard for the consequence of a few forests and villages. Hundreds of millions of innocents have died in senseless wars and at the hands of mindless dictatorships because the human genome chooses self-willed diversity and capital gain over precious human life. Authority guards itself with the blood of those employed to do its bidding, so what's a few forests in the light of so much to gain?

CHAPTER TWO

THE IRON RULE

The Lamb and the Beast are poetical representations of the conflict between the governments of Caesar and the rise of Christianity. In AD 96, Rome's 144 years of iron rule began to deteriorate with the death of the twelfth supreme commander, Domitian. His sudden end came the same way as did that of his six predecessors—by the hand of his compatriots. Although the sun was already setting on this dictatorial form of government, the empire continued for centuries through successful reforms.

As the chief persecutor of the Christians was removed from office, solace came to Rome's greatest nemesis, and John the apostle was released from prison on the Isle of Patmos. Being allowed to return to his church in Ephesus, he took back to his home church more than he had left with. Captivity was most favorable for this old general; he had time to hear from Him whom he served and received the final and most notable Scripture, the book of Revelation.

A hundred years earlier, the third of the twelve eminent rulers, Caesar Augustus, had received the illustrious title merited only by great Roman leaders, Pater Patriae, "Father of the Country." He served fifty-five years as Caesar, the father of the dictators. Like all nervous sovereigns, the Roman emperors secured their offices with spies throughout all their domains.

But this one they never saw coming. Caesar, the Senate, and all the governors had no knowledge of the event that was brewing—the birth of Jesus Christ, who would become the empire's greatest challenge. Jesus was born in humble fashion, but His shepherd's staff ultimately destroyed the iron rule of the Romans. He was not the Father of his country but the "Lord of Lords and King of Kings" (Revelation 17:14).

The word of Caesar controlled all trade, philosophy, culture, and religion. It was a time when one man ruled the masses, so his name was affectionately handed down to his successors. Death and life were in his mouth; any challenge to his throne was brutally crushed. Ironically, the greatest challenge to its power came during Rome's greatest time of strength. Rome's leaders never understood or gave time to consider this challenge; they never thought it would have any merit or right to the throne.

But three hundred years after Jesus' birth came the rise of the Christian faith in the form of Roman sovereignty—the Decree of Constantine. Jesus' humble birth and His death as a criminal resulted in the faith's power and influence that eroded Rome's sovereignty and spread through the world as an unstoppable fire ablaze in faithful hearts. Christianity stood in stark contrast to the tyrants' rule.

Constantine the Great finally surrendered to the Christian faith in AD 313; his predecessors had built on unstable foundations. Though the empire ruled with an iron fist, its heart was full of murder and disloyalty and thus became subject to its own message. Many guards, captains, and servants as well as Constantine turned to the Christian faith for solace.

There is an account recorded around AD 200 of a Roman captain who took pity on one believer being led to martyrdom. This believer transmitted such strong faith and hope to all those in his presence that the captain took pity on him and was envious of his life. The general noticed this reaction and asked him if he would like to die the same way. The captain said he would. After declaring Jesus Christ as his Lord, this tough Roman guard died a martyr as well.

It is supposed that the apostle John returned and served as a bishop of the church at Ephesus as a very old man. It would have been there that John introduced that final installment of arguably the greatest book the world has ever known, "The Revelation of Jesus Christ." In it, he revealed some of Rome's future John had witnessed in his visions—the great struggle between the old sovereign and the new faith.

John would have brought enormous relief and joy to the believers in Asia. History accounts that he just wouldn't die even when they boiled him in oil. Though I have seen no written history about the day of his return, it's possible the church at Ephesus gathered to embrace their longtime friend and brother and the last apostle of Jesus.

The crowd of thousands waited patiently to hear this magnificent but elderly and frail man speak. The silence and stillness of this enormous crowd would have turned his years of suffering into jubilation. From the twelve apostles, the number of believers had grown to number in the thousands. The faith was spreading rapidly through the empire; all attempts to stop or even slow its momentum were failing. The treacherous life of the last of the twelve most prominent of Rome's dictators ended in betrayal and blood; by contrast, the last of the twelve eminent apostles lived out life in triumph and jubilation.

I can see him looking over this transfixed crowd that hungered for his words of encouragement. John unrolled a scroll and began to speak from these last and final famous words of God: "Apokalupsis Ieesou Christou heen edooken autoo ho theos deixai"; "The Revelation of Jesus Christ, which God gave Him to show His servants things which must shortly take place. And He sent and signified it by His angel to His servant John" (Revelation 1:1 NKJV).

The excitement in John's voice as he gave his first message that day would have defied his age of ninety-six. His fears of torture and death would have slipped away like night's shadows in the rising sun. He must have rejoiced as a youthful man in a feast of harvests, jubilant and delighted that this time had arrived. Yet as his loving brethren listened carefully to his every word, they would have had little idea of their significance for the unassuming world yet to be born.

Caesar versus Christ

Was this coincidental that a hundred years earlier, Caesar, the ruler of all the world, was declared a god just as Jesus, the King of the Jews, was born? Was it coincidental that there were twelve kings from Caesar to Domitian (Augustus was two of them; he had ruled as Octavian between 44 BC and 27 BC and as Augustus from 27 BC until AD 14) and twelve apostles? Was it coincidental that these two great periods concluding at the same time?

Christianity began in a spirit of pacifism in sharp contrast to Rome's brutality. Caesar and Christ were opposed in their belief systems, traditions, and lifestyles; they shared no common ground. The lion and the lamb, the fox and the rabbit, the predator and its prey. The Christian faith had no physical sword, no desire to plunder, no desire for conquest. Just as rabbits are defenseless, Christians were.

Was there a more appropriate time for Jesus' birth? Jesus was the antitype of Caesar. While Jesus' blood cried for forgiveness, Caesar's sword cried for blood and revenge. By the sword, Caesar had global authority; he was a god in the Roman pantheon. So too Jesus had a mandate for world rule but not by the sword, not by plunder, but by a new concept. The sword of old was set against this new pacifist movement.

Jesus was about seventeen when Augustus died in AD 14. Augustus's successor, lacking Augustus's character, murdered his rivals to keep his kingdom under control and did so until after Jesus' death. By that time, he had sent Rome on a downward trajectory.

Although they lived like gods, Augustus and Tiberius proved they were not immortals. They had ruled the world and were worshipped as gods, but death still swallowed them. They were men like any other in that they became dust like any other.

By plunder, the Caesars had become givers of life and death, but their influence was only over dominions. Christ turned water into wine and raised the dead. No Caesar could have said, "I come in my Father's Name." John 5:43NKJV

When a Caesar died, he went to the grave, never to return. His legacy remained enshrined in a marble statue, but his flesh was no different from all flesh.

I write not as a historian but as an observer; I am not writing as a professor but as a poet. During these days of old, two titanic forces collided and changed humanity forever. The roots of modern society, religion, commerce, and culture draw from the bedrock of these early days. The hundreds of thousands of humans who died in this clash give satisfactory evidence of these events by the many trophies, emblems, statues, polices, and laws derived from this battle of superpowers two thousand years ago.

All human culture sprouts from the soil of dictatorship, plunder, idol worship, hatred, revelation, salvation, and redemption. The humanists of today have tried to eliminate these riveting reports from our minds. The trees of modernism spring up into the clouds of the final judgment, which will affect us all. Our world is almost out of control; humanity has no more purpose, hope, and justice and perhaps no salvation. All the same, we look for the Savior; it's in our nature to do so.

The ideals of Christ, rebirth, healing, redemption, the battle for world control, and the rise of super antichrist powers emanate from news, sports, cartoons, even politics. We have the fiction of Superman's battles with Lex Luther, John Cena's battles with R-Truth, Batman against the Joker. We have the devastating reality of wars of Hitler versus the Allies, the Taliban against the Western powers, the feud of America with Russia, the battle of the East and the West, democracy versus communism, and left versus right politics.

Honored leaders are modeled on Christ; they can do no wrong. Powerful enemies are built on antichrist ideals; they're bent on evil and world domination. In them, there is no place for change, and imprisonment and death are their means to their wicked ends.

Concepts of redemption cry out in amid the rumble of Roman iron and echo from these foundations. They sprout from the chaos of past ages and rise to take their place in a modern world that mocks the concept of Christ and yet symbolically idolizes the image of Christ.

Fertile ground and flourishing forests are the results of many generations rising and falling, all believing the same and doing the same; we can't avoid our destiny. They speak a poetical proverb: as the flower sprouts from the bud, our genetic code has determined the outcome and is unable to change it.

From treetops, we survey the wonders of the forest, the mighty nations undefeated, indestructible, superior; as gods they reign, as gods they speak, and let all who choose not to follow be afraid. Voices can be heard from the bedrock of the forest; there is a veritable rumbling against the modern ideals that is saying, "Leaves of the great trees born in the mighty forest, you cannot deny us, you came from us. We birthed you; you have now come into being. Because of genetics you exist. Examine your roots; trace your lineage. You came from us, and so your end will be in a similar nature to your beginning."

Insignias of the Past

Our society is the result of our history to a far greater extent than we give it credit for. Our states' crests derive from centuries-old organizational emblems that had relied on entities that predated them by centuries. The English have the royal coat of arms of the United Kingdom. This emblem symbolizes the union of their nation; all the emblems in the crest date to between 1500 and 1700. The lion on the country's coat of arms dates back centuries to the Babylonians, Greeks, and Egyptians. Our concepts of life sciences as well have their origins in Greek philosophy, and our languages were built on past languages. Solomon said, "There is nothing new under the sun," and that is still true today.

Even the infamous Julius Caesar was the product of previous generations. He was not a ruler by birthright but by adoption. He was a mighty warrior chosen by the political elite to show no mercy, tear flesh, murder, and pillage. He was selected to rule and became the seedbed for the mighty, a model, a political genius, and the first of many Caesars.

The human soul was smashed because the mighty were sovereign. From one dark lord rose up dictators for hundreds of years. They were tyrants who used force to rule others. Our history was written by these most dangerous times, and dictators still arise.

The Fairy Tale of Beast Rulers

The Caesar-controlled Roman Empire was symbolized in the book of Daniel as an iron beast. Previous to Caesar, the world powers were symbolized by wild animals—the lion, bear, and leopard. It's ironic that the Bible equates rulers with such wild beasts, but we still do that with our emblems that utilize images of beasts to represent rulers and authority though they are meat-eating animals that prey on us, the lambs. The lion, the bear, and the leopard are ancient symbols of governments East and West, democratic and communist. Lions devour lambs; bears catch salmon; leopards eat deer. They are not symbols of sympathy, empathy, tolerance, or compassion. Such beasts have no love for democracy; they'll not take counsel from the weaker. They rule by their strength; all that is before them is theirs to feast on.

CHAPTER THREE

THE MULTILATERAL WORLD

Societies have become more complex, but they contain vestiges of their foes, those who wielded iron fists. Their governing methods differ; one cries out to capture the terrorist while another cries out to assist the disenfranchised. Over hundreds of years, they've given rise to conflicts and polarized ideals. Our contemporary cosmos is torn between fear and confidence, necessity and humanity, and liberty and protection, and international organizations try to regulate our political ideals and social boundaries.

These global conflicts have a new age of governance, the multilateral world. In previous decades, hundreds of multi- and bilateral organizations have come to be. A world controlled by such organizations is different in nature from that of past totalitarian structures. The goalposts have moved from a one-world concept to the multilateral world. No longer are we seeing one-world dictatorship, one-world government, or one-world currency but a complex organization. I believe this is a biblical prediction.

Babylon, the final kingdom predicted in the last pages of the Bible, is not a monocracy but a multilateral empire likened to a megaplutocracy whereby all the kings of the world have become rich (Revelation 18:3). It is a magocracy, because by its sorcery all the nations were deceived (Revelation 18:23).

While the one-world ideas are a good, modern-day spin to effect new religious belief systems, that in itself doesn't imply it's the real power behind the throne. Everyone knows that with little exception, money rules the world. Those who have the money lead governments and create the rules. Very often, their methods are discreet. They are the puppet masters.

They are skillful technocrats who have pioneered the world's financial systems on the concepts of ecological systems with their seasonal cycles.

The Perfect Golden Goose

The magical goose that lays golden eggs has become reality. If you're not sure what I'm talking about, check the price you paid for that garment or toaster against the cost to manufacture it, and then check your tax bill. Who is the tree and who is the goose for the harvesters?

In Revelation 18, Babylon ruled the nations of the world. Babylon was the final global government before the end brought about a great change of sovereignty. That is when the Lord Himself appeared to all. Meanwhile, now is the day, and I believe that our present commercial system is very similar to the description in Revelation. We have a complex international trading system connected by code-based technology and conducted by great ships. The enigma to uncover is just how Babylon was said to have fornicated with the kings. This was no physical affair; Babylon was described as a mythical person with no physical body. Rather, Babylon's was a moral transgression, a technical betrayal made by rulers at the cost of the people. It seduced by power and status those who betrayed alongside it and ruled with it.

Instead of the end time being that of one world, one sovereign, one currency, it is a complex, multilateral system of control now developing and overtaking us. We're seeing a combination of many sovereigns who made various agreements for commercial and political policy and for control of complex trading agreements with the ultimate power hidden behind those contracts and those who made them.

Did John See a Multilateral Global World?

Did John see this perfect garden, the entire globe controlled by international contracts among nations? Did he see the enabling force of computers and smart technology? Did he see a day that technology ruled the rich and the poor, the whole world? How could a book written 1,940 years ago have relevance for the modern world? How can we remain unconvinced by this powerful deliberation of a poor Jewish fisherman?

John penned the close of the final holy Scripture by describing in some detail a world to come that for the most looks identical to our world today. Almost two millennia after the prophecy, our society is dependent upon international trade, and all the systems and foundational work are in place to force everyone to trade through a unified, personal identification system. The stage is set. The players are making their moves.

Revelation 18 describes a world built on trade conducted by huge ships. This powerful system was called Babylon, and through a colossal environmental disaster, it was destroyed. Our current, vibrant, international trading system shakes and stock markets crash on any negative environmental news. Our global commercial environment is at the pinnacle of uncertainty and vulnerability as had been foretold.

Revelation 13 describes a trading system that controls all the people on earth with numbers. Such a system exists, and the whole world knows about it 1,940 years after this prophecy. The wherewithal for such a global trading system exists.

The old follower of Jesus was not an educated person; he was a fisherman. He had not been trained in the courts of Caesar or educated in business, war, or governance. All the same, this good old Jewish boy would have known how to market his daily catch. Those in the Middle East engaged in trade. Compared to modern culture, early societies were never so dependent on trading as John describes; countries such as Singapore grow nothing; they depend on imports.

Those in the Middle East during John's time would have caught or grown their own food and traded any surplus. Luxuries such as ivory, gold, and spices mentioned in Revelation 18 would have been purchased from traveling merchants by only kings, rulers, and the rich, but nobody was totally dependent on trading.

Yet this old fisherman wrote of the time when the whole world would become interdependent and codependent on merchants. Augustus, the greatest of all the Caesars, would never have dreamed of such an empowering time. If he had had that option, he would have utilized our advanced technologies to impose his authority upon all and extracted everything he could without mercy.

John would have known the history of Rome and its legacy of domination, but the vision he wrote about was not to be fulfilled for generations. Over eighteen hundred years later, the computer age was born when the Babbage calculator was created. Electricity took the world by storm, and this was followed by the invention of vacuum tubes and computer chips. Technology has empowered the greatest of all merchandising in far greater measure than any of the Roman Caesars would have imagined or have been able to orchestrate.

While Julius Caesar had control of the Roman senate, his army, and his populace, he never had control of every transaction, every trade, and every payment gateway. His tax collectors could never know what exactly the taxpayers owed; they relied on force, trickery, and deceit to collect every last dollar they could. John foresaw a time when full commercial control would be achieved over the masses throughout the entire earth.

> He causes all, both small and great, rich and poor, free and slave, to receive a mark on their right hand or on their foreheads, and that no one may buy or sell except one who has the mark or the name of the beast, or the number of his name. (Revelation 13:16–17 NKJV)

We are living in a day when such a system could easily be implemented, and then the rich and the poor will face equal challenges. Maybe those in the middleclass have been easy to manage because of their innate honesty, but the very rich and the very poor will soon have similar difficulties. Governments concentrate on ruling and taxing the middle class because they can't fight the system. The rich can afford to fight the system, while the poor have nothing to give the system except their labor.

The technology needed to make such a system that could control the whole world would need to be very sophisticated. Today, our planet is one big cyber world that has connected billions of gadgets and has dominated businesses and households alike.

Try Ruling the Rich

Robert Kiyosaki, who wrote *Rich Dad, Poor Dad*, explained how society has two systems, one for the rich and one for the poor. He wrote about how to step up from the poor system to the rich system. He claimed that the rich have different financing and tax benefits than do the poor or the middle class because the latter two aren't rich.

Times are changing. Governments are seeking additional sources of revenue beyond what they can collect from the compliant middle classes, and the rich are losing their indemnity to prosecution for white-collar crimes of cooking the books, understating their incomes, and faking financial losses for tax benefits. In New Zealand, some former lofty ones are doing jail time for misleading investors.

But John did not write solely about embezzlers; he foresaw a world in which the rich and the poor played on a level field; the rich would need a mark in order to trade. Could this happen to the rich as it does to the middle class, which bears the heaviest financial burdens of governments because of its members' compliant nature?

The rich will not be able to hide no matter how far they run because technology will track them. Science fiction writer Elizabeth Moon wrote that if it were up to her, every person at birth would be bar coded with a permanent ID number or receive an implant with the same. This technology is being used with domestic animals. Did John write about a time when all humans would be equal in this respect?

Can the rich avoid this? There is a new wave of freedom fighters, geeks who ride on their technological abilities. There's big money on the table, but are the rich losing? Has money lost its gleam?

Mr. Kim Dotcom, born Kim Schmitz, believed his multimillion-dollar file-sharing website, Megaupload, was perfectly legal. Well, Kim didn't make the rules; that was his downfall. He settled in New Zealand, which he discovered to be the land of milk, honey, and police dropping out of the sky during a dawn raid. Ever since, he's been fighting a legal battle against deportation to the United States to face copyright crime.

For federal lawmakers, win or lose may be of no consequence. Maybe they've already won as they've sent a clear message to the e-commerce world that the virtual world of code and copyright belongs to them. By every long arm of the law available to them, they're going to disenfranchise any cavalier activity at any cost and demand payment and conformity to their statutes.

The humble fisherman who looked down through 1,940 years penned this correctly. We have solid evidence that the rich are losing their ability to be exempt from the rules; the powerful ax of the law will fall on them as it does on everyone else.

CHAPTER FOUR

THE IMPACT OF TECHNOLOGY

Ruling the Poor by Technology

There had never been a time when the poor were not lorded over. Every society has that structure. In Western countries, these systems are controlled by the government's social support offices, which use tax revenues to assist the poor. Yet only about 20 percent of the world's population of 7 billion have the luxury of government-assisted social services.

Within developing countries and many non-Western countries, social support comes from within the community, often through systems far outside direct government control. Some social support takes the form of humanitarian efforts from societies and individuals. My friend Prakash talked about a mission to reach the villages of India; in 1997, there were some 700,000 villages, only 10 percent of which had any kind of Western infrastructure and support. Hundreds of thousands of those villages had no electricity or even roads. Many had never seen a Westerner let alone a telephone or any other advanced technology.

These village people are in the group of the poorest in the world. Estimated at over a billion in number, they live in dire need with earnings of under US$1 a day. A larger group lives on less than US$2.50 a day. These figures are staggering; modern technology and trading techniques control over 85 percent of the world's wealth, but there seems little that can be given back to the majority stakeholders of this human genome.

The biggest stumbling to the words of John, if there can ever be such a global system of control, is this statement: "He causes all, both small and great, rich and poor, free and slave, that no one may buy or sell except"

(Revelation 13:16–17 NKJV paraphrased). These words about the poor need full consideration. The 3 billion humans living on less than US$2.50 a day are included in these prophetic words. There is a difficulty with this group because no government or corporation will bother coming up with the investments to control them.

By comparison, a member of the middle class pay for their system of control and are doing so more and more online. They bank, vote, trade, pay bills, file taxes, and communicate online, and the costs of the infrastructure to achieve these time-saving benefits are paid for by the users. They are wired and connected enough to buy their gadgets online and pay for them the same way. The poor don't have it that easy.

The more privileged village people have the luxury of living in city villages. Their houses are identical, and they all have the same satellite dishes on their roofs and the same motor scooters out front. The families live in a single room where they watch TV and eat. In some way, the families of the poor combine earnings to scale up the ladder of that terrible pyramid from bottom feeding to a life of some dignity, so they can leave something for their children. The first and most crucial step up is their education.

My visit to India showed me the world is surely on that path described by John. The control of people through their financial transactions works only if they have something to give; a dollar a day will not pay for their administration. But the poor are not remaining poor because technology is bringing them hope. As global initiatives push for a better tomorrow, the possibilities of education, global awareness, and equal opportunity are awaking the disadvantaged. A new middle class is springing up in Asia, India, Africa, and elsewhere.

To help make this happen, second- and third-generation technology is being remanufactured and distributed to the multitudes in the villages that is connecting them to the world cheaply. My daughter went on a missionary trip to Russia and was surprised to see even the youngest had cell phones.

In 2007, about 4 billion people owned cell phones, a technology that has impacted developing countries in particular. Today, over 5.6 billion people use cell phones worldwide. If the world truly has 3 billion people earning under US$2.50 a day, some of them are using cell phones in spite of their poverty. In just four years, cell phone usage has increased by over 1.5 billion in developing countries. China has led the way in reducing the number of those in poverty (those living on less than US$1 a day) from 85 percent of the population to 16 percent; some 600 million people there are now earning more than US$2.50 a day due to the industrial boom in China.

John's prophecy seems to have some potential for fulfillment even in the face of global impoverishment. Not only is it happening, but every commercial and global organization wants it to happen.

The Emerging Garden of Smart Technology

At the beginning of the twentieth century, the Western world relied on a telephone system run by operators and manual switchboards. People purchased Victrolas to listen to records, and the post–World War I era witnessed rapid change as radios helped people stay informed. The well-to-do enjoyed these three items of technology.

In between the two terrible world wars, many new manufacturing industries were created in areas such as aviation and engineering. Technology boomed and formed giant companies such as IBM, Motorola, and Boeing. After World War II, these companies diversified and started producing for the new and growing domestic markets. This is perhaps when the age of consumerism began. In his paper "Price Competition in 1955," Victor Lebow wrote,

> Our enormously productive economy demands that we make consumption our way of life that we convert the buying and use of goods into rituals that we seek our spiritual satisfaction and our ego satisfaction in consumption. We want things consumed, burned up, worn out, replaced and discarded at an ever-increasing rate. (Quote from Journal of Retailing, by *Victor Lebow 1955*)

Throughout Europe and America, it became fashionable in the sixties to buy radios, vacuums, washing machines, and all types of household innovations. It was a time when living was appreciated and uncomplicated. Technology was becoming the foundation of a quality of life that had never been experienced before. Just think of the advent of TV and the drive to buy television sets.

One television, one telephone, one car per household. One new vacuum cleaner replacing an older model, and an automatic washing machine replacing the old wringer-washer. In the sixties, houses doubled the number of technological marvels.

Throughout the seventies and the eighties, *micro* became the buzzword. Though transistors had been invented earlier, these silicon devices allowed prices and sizes of what had been luxury items to drop drastically and pave the way for such must-have items as Sony's Walkman.

In the nineties, Mom and Dad each had cell phones while the kids played on Atari or Sega game consoles and listened to music on CDs and watched movies on videotape. They used food processors, sandwich makers, and microwave ovens, and they used personal computers at least at the office and frequently at home.

It used to be that technological advances were measured in terms of items per household; now, they are being measured in terms of items per person.

Now and the Coming 2020s

The European Organization for Nuclear Research (the former CERN) was the early instigator of the World Wide Web. It proposed a code, hypertext markup language (HTML), to connect all researchers. This development formed the backbone of the Internet in the mid-1990s. By the end of the twentieth century, this development had grown to global significance.

In the early period of the new age of that great decade, Microsoft, Apple, and Open Source were developing intuitive computing platforms that even children found easy to use. Soon, the whole earth was connected, but then the greatest development was still yet to take place. It was first released in China. People lined up for hours to buy the first iPhones, which incorporated everything learned from the past.

By 2020, the world will be full of these smart handhelds, but that will come with a price. All who use such smart devices will be subject to invasions of their privacy and degradation of their human rights that Revelation predicted. Those who use smart devices broadcast their exact location every time they are on, and intelligence organizations store all their information. Someone knows what toothpaste we use, how much we spend daily, and how much we eat not to mention where we live.

Think about this: one day, it could become a crime for turning your device off or not having it on your person. That day could arrive before we have time to wake up. Maybe it will be the rumor of an alien invasion with stories of people disappearing. Therefore, such laws could start in small countries, but they will be adopted by others, and pretty soon, all countries will have similar laws: throw your smart device away and enforcers suddenly drop out of helicopters to arrest you.

The smart benefits will always weigh in the favor of the publisher: smart personal identification to stop ID theft, smart synchronization with home or business devices, smart locator on your social network. But the desire for subversive smart metadata from every user will ultimately trump every smart device. Maybe in these days, a large portal such as Facebook will become mandatory as a global compositor of all human identities. On April 15, 2013, Google's boss said that the entire world would be online by 2020.

John's Technology Prediction

Did the old fisherman from Galilee make a plausible prediction? Will there come a time when the system controls everyone, rich and poor alike? There's a growing realism that such things are more than just "on the horizon." Human resistance could be the only barrier. Many technologies could constitute violations of human rights, but in my opinion, the multilateral Babylon will have that problem covered. People won't realize their rights are being violated. These new technologies could be touted as humanity's greatest achievement as a way to coax humanity into a new era.

CHAPTER FIVE

THE GLOBAL CITY

One City to Rule Them All

John's community was most likely a group of simple fishermen. One day, Jesus of Nazareth walked through his town and John's life changed radically. Fifty years after meeting Jesus, John penned the final book of the greatest book, the Bible.

Within the concluding chapters of this controversial and epic journey, John laid claim to the destruction of some megacity called Babylon, a city described to represent the trading, commerce, and banking activity of the nations. It was a financially flourishing metropolis trading in an endless supply of worldwide luxuries.

A key phrase that John alluded to is in direct contrast to the construct of the old dictatorial governance he was raised in. The strong arm of Caesar, John's supreme ruler of his day, stretched throughout the known world with unmerciful force. His army was bringing all peoples to their knees. Many despised his iron fist; plenty of people made plans to take Caesar down. His closest allies took the throne by force; Julius was assassinated, but seven out of the eleven Caesars' to follow died the same way.

The leadership of that day was vile and cruel; grown men went through Bethlehem, swords drawn, slaying all the baby boys under age two. Mothers pled and fathers grieved as the soldiers carried out their command. They killed innocents with no regard for the value of human souls. The slaying in Bethlehem, known by all the world, was typical of this ruthless generation. This murderous genocide escaped any consequence in human terms (Matthew 2:16).

Similar military dictators today aren't as successful in taking brutal control with little regard to the human plight without facing the consequences. Hussein and Gaddafi had no place to hide; Mladic's crimes resulted in his downfall. How much longer before the fall of al-Asaad?

When John wrote, the countries of the old world were not like those today, but he described the future accurately. John predicted a kingdom that would control the world not by force but by trade. This was in complete opposition to everything John had experienced. He had been in prison because of such brutal rulers, yet he foresaw a day when the leaders of the world would be bound to each other not by extreme force but by the desire to trade; they would be bound by multilateral contracts, collective organizations, agreements—small and large nations alike. "The kings of the earth have committed fornication with her, and the merchants of the earth have become rich through the abundance of her luxury" (Revelation 18:3b NKJV) and "The kings of the earth who committed fornication and lived luxuriously with her" (Revelation 18:9a NKJV).

Multilateral Babylon

John would have been amazed that his vision was in radical contrast to his personal reality. In his life, people were controlled by pain and the fear of death; he was in a labor camp that worked prisoners to death. Yet John saw in his visions a world to come controlled by pleasures and extravagance. So voluptuous was this world that the kings and rulers couldn't avoid the pleasures it brought to them. John's generation was controlled by pain; the generation he saw that was to come was controlled by the allure of wicked pleasure.

"The kings of the earth who committed fornication and lived luxuriously with her." The Greek word for *fornication* is the basis of our word *porn*, but physical impurity wasn't the issue. The fornication was with Babylon, a city. Kings are by birthright or election supposed to rule their people justly and morally, but the kings in John's revelation will not be like them.

Conflict of Interest

In modern times, these kings are our presidents, prime ministers, mayors, governors, ministers, and in some countries generals. They are generally elected to govern with no conflicts of interest; they are not to bow to manipulation, coercion, or greed. At least Western democracy holds such standards whether by signed documents or by conventional thinking; its rulers are not to use their influence for personal profit or benefit.

John foresaw a time when the world's rulers would choose to ally with multiple systems that create secret conflicts of interest; they commit adultery in this respect by having clandestine "relations" with other bodies even if they are simply governmental bodies. They sign nondisclosure agreements to protect their private dealings and keep the public in the dark.

Jesus said that no one could serve God and Mammon (Luke 16:13) and related this fact to adultery (Luke 16:18). The leaders of His time were under an oath to God to serve the people, but they had decided to serve the world and money rather than have mercy on their people. They committed adultery with their offices when they violated their oaths.

Clearly, not all rulers of our modern metropolises are so corrupt, but they have all signed nondisclosure agreements, and while it is impossible to rule without such contracts, the point of John's prophecy is that all the nations would be ruled by such conflicting loyalties.

The Conflict with Babylon

The Babylon John described didn't exist in AD 95, but a great city called Babylon is recognized by all historians; its global significance peaked about 700 years previously. The mighty King Nebuchadnezzar dominated the known world and established Babylon's golden years, but it soon fell to other kingdoms that were jostling for global power themselves.

It was one the greatest ancient cities; it lasted a few thousand years until falling to the Persians in 539 BC. Its remains lie in the battlefields of Iraq. Some are upset the Americans placed their Alpha base on top of Saddam Hussein's attempt to raise up the ancient ruins to a modern metropolis. His sudden end stopped any work at the site.

The ancient meaning of the word *Babylon* is "confusion" and comes from the word *babel*. Genesis 11 deals with a post-apocalyptic phase of humanity. The trend of huddling in communities gave way to the idea of a super city. These people wanted to build a name for themselves and become great. They attempted to build a city with a tower so high it would reach the heavens.

When God checked out this super structure, He possibly decided that humanity's impressive ability to build anything or do anything they desired would lead to a whole lot of trouble. He instantly undercut humanity's ability to communicate by making them speak different languages (Genesis 11:9). On that day, confusion fell on all humanity; it was the second great catastrophe that had befell them in less than a hundred years. The tower therefore was called Babel because of the confusion.

Did John see a new city rising from the ancient dust of the original mega city? Or was he referring to another city or a global metropolis? Would a world of mixed ethnicities, languages, and mutual indifference coalesce in a virtual city on the Internet?

A city of 10 million or more is a mega city; there are twenty-six in the world. Tokyo, at 34 million, is the largest. Though some mega cities such as New York and London have some characteristics of John's Babylon, they're not quite all encompassing, and there is no one that truly rules them all. According to John, this will be a city of physical substance that will fall in one hour in an earthquake (Revelation 16:19). Will this be an actual city?

That Great City Babylon

Though we don't have such a Babylon today, one could be built, and an earthquake could destroy it. Why would such a city be built? What would be the benefits? We have so many well-established super cities already, so why another? It would be a city that housed world organizations and possibly become sovereign. Currently, there are many ancient cities that are prominent for trade and diplomacy.

Many powerful entities have headquarters in Geneva, Brussels, Washington, DC, and New York. There are more than 300 unique world organizations. Most likely, the greatest of world organizations with incredible multinational power is the United Nations. Based in New

York, it employs some 5,000 staff there and 60,000 worldwide. Does this influence make New York the Babylon of Scripture, the center of globalization and worldly governance?

Manhattan's seven World Trade Center buildings are being rebuilt. Does this seven match the seven heads of the Beast? Could they represent the seven mountains? Could they represent the one-world government of the future (which I believe is more of a smoke screen)? One of the twin towers, the Freedom Tower, has been renamed One World Trade Center. I think this is a page to keep watch on.

These massive World Trade Towers seem to be associated in some way to the developing of international organizations; the idea of a city entirely established for international affairs would be particularly compelling. Possibly, such a city would need to be founded similar in nature to that of Vatican City, a nation unto itself. Vatican City was established in 1929 and is a walled enclave in Rome. It is the smallest sovereign state in the world. It has its own government, bank, mayor, and even an international football team.

Possibly, Manhattan, already a kind of city in a city and the abode of the seven World Trade Towers, could become sovereign as Vatican City is and have its own governance, give out its own passports, and more important have indemnity from contractual obligations.

The Seven Organizations of the Global City

As well as the United Nations, there are seven main groups of International organizations.

- Multilateral institutions (the United Nations is the largest)
- European Union institutions
- International Monetary Fund
- World Bank
- World Trade Organization
- regional development banks
- international nongovernmental organizations

I have listed them to show there are seven types of global groups. Apart from the number seven, I am not sure of the global significance to Revelation.

A City Sovereign

These seven types of global organizations are involved in global affairs of money and wealth distribution and the movement of goods between nations. Our world has become incredibly complex and codependent on trade between countries; the new global organizations help resolve differences and secure continuity between trading partners.

I suggest that governments have signed contracts with such global organizations that can at times conflict with the affairs of those sovereign governments. It was publicly reported some years ago that the United Nations asked New Zealand to change some of its social laws. The way they were changed locally was subversive; not once while the changes were being proposed was there any mention of UN involvement. Still today, most New Zealanders disagree with the outcome the UN wanted.

A sovereign nation was reported to have failed in securing a multimillion-dollar refunding through the World Bank because of its attempt to constitute policy not accepted by the UN. These multilateral agreements are mostly about trade agreements. Just how the UN is involved in trade I'm not sure, but the outcomes are easily discovered.

John saw this great city Babylon fostering worldwide wealth through its luxuries. Never before has there been a time of such luxury, comfort, leisure, and pleasure for so many nations; such addictive fruits result in many inhumane laws. I believe the multilateral system helps maintain immoral financial imbalance between nations.

The whole world is being plugged into the wealth machine. Power and technology enable humans to derive benefits beyond their wildest dreams; even a common modern house is more luxurious than what kings, princes, and lords lived in just two hundred years ago. We have clean heat in well-insulated homes and soft carpet under our feet. We no longer have to chop wood to heat houses with cold stone floors. We no longer have to saddle up and ride miles to deliver messages on cold nights. We watch TV while we soak in bubbling hot tubs and tweet our thoughts to the world. And these luxuries are not just for the rich; they are the possessions of the masses.

Road to Babel

Are these the luxuries John saw? Nations' economies are now dependent on the revenues produced by all the manufacturing and developments in technology. The winds of business confidence change within hours, even minutes, of news that centuries before would have taken months to affect an economy. Now in under a minute, stock markets and currencies can go up or down based on a news report.

Metadata is the term given to the massive amounts of information that is being harvested as a result of the use of electronic devices. Our browsing activity is recorded and used by intelligence groups, unbeknownst to us, to craft the future colors, styles, relationships, wants, and habits we will later indulge in.

Technologies will harvest more information, and global institutions are on the rise. As the Murdoch case in England has shown us, battles between giant media forces and government will continue and personal freedom will be overridden. The information being harvested could give rise to the mother of all governments that crafts laws to limit our freedom.

Globalization is a natural trend; will these seven groups of global political and financial power end up at the top of the pyramid? For these organizations to have direct control over people in any country, they would need to bypass the sovereign power of that country. This can happen, as the NSA is proving, whether the sovereign stays in control or collapses.

Maybe it's an age-old dream locked in the heart of humanity that forever repeats itself as in the movie *Ground Hog Day*; we awake to repeat what we did yesterday. This is the path to Babel, an ancient call beyond the realm of reason to build skyscrapers. The hope remains that if we build large enough and tall enough, if our dreams can reach what our eyes behold, we will create a utopia that the gods themselves will honor.

We live in a time when nations have been reborn in a day. Israel and Iraq were given their constitutions by the League of Nations in 1917. Suddenly, people who had lost their ethnic sovereign identities became nations again. South Sudan, the world's newest nation, comprises ten states in Africa. In a few years, life dramatically changed for this breakaway from Sudan and Egypt as 8 million people gained their own international identity.

Maybe it's possible for a new mega city to rise from the dust. Maybe Babylon will be created. Urbanization in China has resulted in four hundred new cities being created in the last thirty years complete with multiplexes and highways and problems for their elderly struggling to adapt to Western lifestyles.

Super cities are forming as a natural trend of globalization as economies and business centers of governing bodies combine resources to create larger bureaucracies to become more viable internationally. But can a mega city be purposely built? Will Babylon rise from oblivion, from a purposeful plan to rule the nations to be the city of cities, the headquarters of all global entities?

Only time will tell. All the same, it seems that most nations are on the road to Babel as complexity and confusion increase. Maybe the nexus will be that one software system that makes sense of everything and brings relief to our worn-out human brains.

Monocracy versus Multipartition

The nations are on the shores of new systems of controls as they're beginning to be ruled by multinational entities, a complex intermingling of governments and commerce to overcome trade, language, and ethnic barriers. I see these multilateral agreements as Revelation's end-time government though this would appear to be opposed to the contemporary idea that there will be a single government, a monocracy ruling in the last days.

The revelator saw all the kings in adultery with this mega city. In modern speak, they were secretly in bed with this government partner. That could have been addressing the modern movement toward secret agreements never made public or disseminated on a "need to know" basis. Commercial necessity has trumped honesty, deceit is on the rise, world leaders sign agreements their people have no idea about, and consecutive governments feel obliged to honor these previously signed documents. This is the model I see John giving in Revelation 17 and 18.

If, on the other hand, the final state of the earth was to be a one-world government, the capital would be Babylon, a monocracy. But that's not how it was written, and it's certainly not how it's happening in the world today.

Multinationals contracted by multilateral agreements through their governments could be more-binding agendas than the national agreements they first vowed to serve, and this gives rise to conflicts of interest. The leaders, ministers, governors, prime ministers, and the like, after successfully screwing up or improving their countries for purposes never disclosed, could end up ruling the earth through multilateralism. These ideals wouldn't survive a single global bureaucracy as some suggest will happen, but they flourish in the growing economy of the rising multipartite globalization.

Where there was never a generation in the past that could have created a single city to rule the world, now, with our complex mix of media, banking, diplomacy, and technology, this is now possible. Whether virtual or solid brick, whether in New York or split among three, seven, or even ten cities, the groundwork is there to make this happen. Maybe such a city already rules the world. Maybe a Babylon exists.

What more could we learn of this great city? Who are its governors? Which organizations are in bed with which globalists? Who runs this polyeconomy? What technology will be used?

CHAPTER SIX

THE RULE OF NUMBERS

The Perfect Commercial and Ecosystem
Is Controlled by Numbers

What could be the crowning enigma concerning this mysterious book Revelation is a prediction that these magnificent and mighty days we live in will be controlled and ruled by numbers. They are mostly unseen, but they have such an incredible impact on our lives.

In Revelation 13:16–18, John revealed that it was by a system of numbers that the rulers of darkness were revealed. How could John have possibly predicted such an outcome? The computer programs and numbers that control us exist in virtual darkness. Could darkness rule us through these same numbers? They can control lives and raise up and pull down people, even countries. Because of unfavorable numbers, people jump from tall buildings to their deaths. By numbers, multilateral agreements are signed, and thousands of news articles produce fear throughout all nations. Numbers rule trading, banking, interest rates, GDPs, turnover, profit, losses, personal wealth, income, and demographic statistics.

Numbers dictate the worth of each person. Nations and organizations compare wealth based on numbers. When the numbers are good, the people rejoice. When the numbers are bad, the people become depressed.

Though most policy and governance is consumed by the need to make dollar numbers better, the crunching of numbers and the determination of these things are never seen because they happen in a virtual world not understood by most of the people it affects. Economists interpret the multidimensional effects of intermingling currencies and economies and what the results will be to give policymakers insight and vote accordingly.

As a result of 9/11, one bank was destroyed. The records of hundreds of millions of dollars were wiped out and never recovered. Where is your money now? In a virtual account? Just some digits on a computer?

Commerce rules the world, but who is ruling commerce? "Let him who has understanding calculate the number of the Beast, for it is the number of a man: His number is 666" (Revelation 13:18 NKJV). John revealed that evil would rule through a multiplicity of leaders and that their identities would be revealed through numbers.

Computers crunch numbers that make it possible to communicate, trade, and network. Numbers are the critical component of this system. John told us that "by these very numbers" we can uncover the source of the darkness that runs these virtual worlds. Computer codes aren't hidden; anyone can become a programmer. All the same, they operate in darkness 24/7, and hundreds of millions of interconnected computers run our world.

John, who lived thousands of years before the technological era, predicted that a day was coming that computer systems would be synchronized to control and even constrain trade itself. Rich and poor would be subject to these virtual systems whereby people would be unable to trade unless they had a special identifying mark (Revelation 13:16–17), the mark of the Beast. It's staggering that a fisherman 2,000 years ago could write such powerful words that would affect this generation of 7 billion operating in this complex commercial economic system. Yet many of the same group would gladly mock and scorn the thought of these ancient writings having any relevance to or influence on their thinking.

We live among a generation of super intellectual beings some of whom treat Christians with disdain and disgust, but it's becoming increasingly difficult to ignore these powerful, Christian-based predictions that are being fulfilled before our eyes. We have become the witnesses of pure numbers controlling our destiny.

Numbers reveal those who hide behind others. The numbers that calculate this have been hidden in letter-number codes of our English version of the Bible for 400 years now. In a world that runs by computer codes, it should be no surprise that a simple code in Scripture was undiscovered for decades.

As the great day approaches, John's prophecies take on even greater importance. He was John the fisherman, John the revelator, John the friend of Jesus. Even modern literalists such as Elizabeth Moon could well have said, "Give everyone a number so they can trade."

Every new development in modern technology is just another nail in the coffin of those who mock Christianity and resist the idea that the Bible was given to us by a holy God. They can mock, but the outcome will remain the same: the unstoppable and ultimate system of individual control.

The world and its inhabitants are traveling rapidly toward a multipartite totality, a unification of democracies and plutocracies through multilateralism in which maybe even the air we breathe will be proportioned. It is happening now, and every new development is another brick in our Tower of Babel. There is nothing Babylon can't achieve, including reaching the stars and harnessing the foundations of the universe.

#Mr. Smith told Neo, "Listen to the sound of inevitability"; the outcome is inevitable because it's in our nature. It is likewise the nature of the Beast to control the world.

The Beast Has a Code

"Here is wisdom. Let him who has understanding calculate the number of the Beast, for it is the number of a man: His number is 666" (Revelation 13:18 NKJV). The Beast is more than a person living during the life span of a single human generation.

> Then I stood on the sand of the sea. And I saw a beast rising up out of the sea, having seven heads and ten horns, and on his horns ten crowns, and on his heads a blasphemous name. Now the beast which I saw was like a leopard, his feet were like the feet of a bear, and his mouth like the mouth of a lion. The dragon gave him his power, his throne, and great authority. (Revelation 13:1–2 NKJV)

This Beast has a lot going on. If the seven heads are not a giveaway, consider its four natures. The beast is in one body but represents many identities: a lion, a bear, and a leopard with dragon power. The identities have seven heads with ten horns each with a crown. (For this book, we're paying interest only to the entities.)

"Let him who has Wisdom Count"; at the end of chapter 13, John tells us to count its number. "Here is wisdom. Let him who has understanding calculate the number of the beast, for it is the number of a man: His number is 666" (Revelation 13:18 NKJV).

The word *count* in some translations is written as "calculate," yet in Greek, it's a word that means "counting pebbles as used in voting." This is not rocket science. Revelation 13:18 also shows us that the number of the beast is the number of man: 666. John's mystery begins to unfold.

The quadripartite comprises four entities. The Beast consists of and is equal to the union of the lion, bear, leopard, and dragon, including ten horns and ten crowns (Revelation 13:1–2). This union of four is the principal construct of the Beast; it could have a different number of heads or horns or crowns but it would still be a composite of four beasts; it would have the mouth of a lion, the appearance of a leopard, the feet of a bear, and the power of a dragon.

What I have discovered is a number-letter pattern to this union of four that calculates with perfect symmetry and points to the purpose. The Beast = the union of four = 666.

666, Mathematics, and Translations

"Here is wisdom. Let him who has understanding calculate the number of the Beast, for it is the number of a man: His number is 666" (Revelation 13:18 NKJV). The word *understanding* refers to the encryption in the Bible that can be deciphered.

English Language

The following decryption is based on English, the world language, rather than on Greek or Hebrew. As mentioned already, it's believed that God confused all the languages, a sign He owns them all. I'm not sure why this letter cypher works in English considering the Scriptures were written in Hebrew and Greek; it's a sign and a wonder. God must have decided that English would end up the most dominant language.

The letter-number cipher assigns a numerical value to each letter: a = 1, b = 2, and so on, all the way to z = 26. Associating letters and numbers goes way back. Hebrew, Greek and Latin all assigned numerical equivalents to letters. The enigma this book explains is that decoding the Beast is made possible through analyzing these unions of four by letter-number cyphers based on the King James English translation of 1611.

Here is the English translation of the Greek: "Let him that hath understanding (echoon noun) count the number of the Beast (pseefisatoo ton arithmon tou threeiou) number for of a man (arithmos gar anthroopou) it is and number his six hundred threescore and six (estin, kai ho arthmos autou hexakosioi hexeekonta hex). Note the exceptionally clear language: "count the number" and "number for a man."

Men and beasts have names that are collections of letters all of which have numerical equivalents. The numbers of the Beast total 666. By adding the numerical equivalents of the letters of a name, we can determine that *Caesar* equals 47.

$$c = 3, a = 1, e = 5, s = 19, a = 1, r = 18$$

The calculation of wisdom is as uncomplicated as this; it's the sum of the union of four. Revelation 13:8 concludes with the word *wisdom* (*nous* in Greek), something we can aspire to when it comes to the number 666 and its significance.

The Calculation Benchmarks

The calculations will look like this: (4 entities) of (A = 1 ~ Z = 26) = 666, the number of the beast being like a lion, a bear, a leopard, and a dragon. The union of four entities must total exactly 666.

The four names that add up to 666 need to have a relationship equal to the original Scripture patterns as given; otherwise, the conclusion is misleading. For example, the names of random people found in the phone directory could total 666, but this proves nothing, as these random names have no connection to the subject at hand. All calculations need to identify with the cause unambiguously. No one person or institutions deserve to be identified with things with which they are not affiliated.

Who Is the Beast? (Revelation 13)

According to Scripture, he is well known in the earth by these seven attributes.

- wounded but healed
- marveled upon
- feared in war
- worshipped
- has limited power over the saints
- has total global authority
- practices deception

All calculations should agree with these seven attributes to some measure or we're just chasing the wind.

The Discovery

I first discovered this about twenty years ago. Originally, I was calculating longhand. I would write out words and their numerical values looking for that union of 666. I had made one significant discovery whereby each entity had something relevant to world dominion. Though amazed, I held to the idea as only plausible.

Later, a friend wrote a computer program that would translate the values of letters, and that led to my discovery of many of these unions that totaled 666. I was careful to stick to biblical words in Scripture so my findings would be credible.

While I was researching the Scriptures on good Bible software, Revelation 17:3–5 caught my attention because it had a pattern of three plus one.

> So he carried me away in the Spirit into the wilderness. And I saw a woman sitting on a scarlet **Beast** which was full of names of blasphemy, having seven heads and ten horns. The woman was arrayed in purple and scarlet, and

adorned with gold and precious stones and pearls, having in her hand a golden cup full of abominations and the filthiness of her fornication. And on her forehead a name was written: MYSTERY, **BABYLON THE GREAT, THE MOTHER OF HARLOTS AND OF THE ABOMINATIONS OF THE EARTH. "Emphasis added"**

This Beast in Revelation chapter 17 appears to be the same Beast as in chapter 13. A woman is riding the Beast, and three names are written on her forehead. It jumped out— three names on the beast—three plus one, the pattern of four. *No way!* I thought. It couldn't be that simple.

I was shaking at the discovery. Three names were on the woman, and the fourth was the Beast. I thought that if this doesn't calculate, it's all wrong. It was like finding a jewel while strolling the beach. My mind was in doubt while my heart experienced joy. While the woman's representation was significant, the calculation had a veritable wow factor.

CHAPTER SEVEN

CONCLUSION

From the dawn of a new age, John saw forward through hundreds of years of progressive civilizations to a perfect, golden system by which all the rulers of the world would become exceedingly rich. Babylon ruled over all kingdoms on earth. That is John's word: "They were made Rich" by this multilateral system superior to any before. It was established for maximum profit from trading goods and currencies, and it catered to the inhumane unbalance between a certain quality of life and those who wanted it.

In essence, it holds all its elements at arm's length to maintain a critical balance between everything within its control and thereby continues to create extreme disproportion in wealth. Doesn't the world have many organizations to help the poor and reduce inequality? The world does have such institutions, but why are they so ineffective?

If there were a fair global system that produced equality of life, wealth, and justice, consumerism would be doomed. The current world economy would collapse because equality would destroy the world markets and throw the world back five hundred years. I'd prefer equality, but I don't think it's possible to achieve.

The multilateral system is the way the earth copes with these extreme inequalities; to let the rich become richer. We've all heard of overnight millionaires; our system is working well for the rich, but is it also the picture John described? This multifaceted beast is ruling the planet, and it does not have a single color or a single head or a single horn. It doesn't look like a single animal either. John saw a multiplicity of natures, types, heads, and horns—multiple sovereignties—joined in a single body (Revelation 13).

The Beast that comprised aspects of a lion, bear, leopard, and dragon represented successive world powers that dominated the earth for centuries. The seven heads referred to seven different natures and places of authority. Outwardly, these seven could look to be in disharmony and warring against each other. They could look like different seasons of humanity not working together. Then suddenly they're old friends signing deals and shaking hands, and we're left wondering what's going on.

The Beast that controls these political powers and rulers has one purpose in mind, and the powers are controlled by this system far beyond their individual abilities to resist. This system has one ultimate goal that was around since Jesus' time: to destroy the followers of Jesus Christ (Revelation 12–13).

Does this mean every person involved in governments or global organizations must be in opposition to the Christian movement? No. Everyone in this system has the freedom and ability to serve God, follow Jesus, and walk in a godly manner.

Daniel served the kingdoms of Babylon and Media-Persia, and in his days, he was loyal to evil and good kings alike. Daniel was a godly prophet and a righteous man. Daniel wrote his prophetic message while serving a wicked kingdom. God never held Daniel accountable for the decisions and lifestyles of his superiors.

If God can protect a man like Daniel and keep him in a place of authority in spite of the gross abominations of his leaders in the old covenants, how much more can He do for you in a new and glorious covenant of Jesus Christ? Don't be afraid of this system. It will not suddenly appear with frightening tyranny and persecution. It is already here. You were born in it, and because of this, you too can succeed in this. You're called to be great, to shine your righteousness on a lost and confused world.

PART 2

CHAPTER EIGHT

THE BEAST OF BABYLON

I was surprised to discover that this 666 system went right through the book of Revelation. In this first example, we see the end of all things, that final destructive global force, the ultimate Beast, that last strongman in any movie or game. This calculation is a benchmark to help us discover other union patterns of four. Here are the four names I have calculated.

The woman rode on a Beast: "So he carried me away in the Spirit into the wilderness. And I saw a woman sitting on a scarlet beast which was full of names of blasphemy, having seven heads and ten horns" (Revelation 17:3 NKJV).

The first word is *Beast*; on the woman's head were three names: "BABYLON THE GREAT, THE MOTHER OF HARLOTS AND OF THE ABOMINATIONS OF THE EARTH" (Revelation 17:5 NKJV). These three plus Beast make four names.

1. Beast
2. Babylon the Great
3. The Mother of Harlots
4. The Abominations of the Earth

These four titles make up a union in a relationship for a purpose. These letters in the titles can be converted to numbers.

Beast

Letter / Number

b = 2, e = 5, a = 1, s = 19, t = 20

Number Value
2 + 5 + 1 + 19 + 20 = **47**

Mother of Harlots

Letter / Number
m = 13, o = 15, t = 20, h = 8, e = 5, r = 18, o = 15, f = 6, h = 8, a = 1, r = 18, l = 12, o = 15, t = 20, s = 19

Number Value
13 + 15 + 20 + 8 + 5 + 18 + 15 + 6 + 8 + 1 + 18 + 12 + 15 + 20 + 19 = **193**

The Abominations of the Earth

Letter / Number
t = 20, h = 8, e = 5, a = 1, b = 2, o = 15, m = 13, i = 9, n = 14, a = 1, t = 20, i = 9, o = 15, n = 14, s = 19, o = 15, f = 6, t = 20, h = 13, e = 5, e = 5, a = 1, r = 18, t = 20, h = 8

Number Value
20 + 8 + 5 + 1 + 2 + 15 + 13 + 9 + 14 + 1 + 20 + 9 + 15 + 14 + 19 + 15 + 6 + 20 + 13 + 5 + 5 + 1 + 18 + 20 + 8 = **271**

Babylon the Great

Letter / Number
b = 2, a = 1, b = 2, y = 25, l = 12, o = 15, n = 14, t = 20, h = 8, e = 5, g = 7, r = 18, e = 5, a = 1, t = 20

Number Value
2 + 1 + 2 + 25 + 12 + 15 + 14 + 20 + 8 + 5 + 7 + 18 + 5 + 1 + 20 = **155**

47 + 193 + 271 + 155 = 666

Summary of the Beast of Babylon

These four unique entities, each being a title, are relevant to the theme in Revelation 13 about world dominion and global authority. In this first union, the titles are directly word for word out of Scripture. The Beast and the woman on the Beast are a picture of the end-times global governments and their style of leadership. Therefore, why would they not add up to 666? I was shaking because it appeared too obvious; for the numbers not to add up would destroy credibility. I was stunned. This union shows the entire end game. Let us look closer at each component.

Beast = 47

Beast is used fourteen times in chapter 13 and thirty-seven times in the book of Revelation. The letters in *beast* adds up to forty-seven, the same number the name *Caesar* adds up to. The early church believed the Beast referred to the Roman Empire, which Caesar ruled. I am not sure there is anything by chance. The Beast was carrying this woman, who represented end-time kingdoms that had their roots in the kingdoms of the Caesars.

Mother of Harlots = 193

This is a terrible title, one I will not explain. The number 193 is the same number as another significant global organization, the Roman Catholic Church. So while it's assumed this refers to an adulteration of religious organizations, why does the Mother of Harlots equal the same as the Roman Catholic Church? Could the Roman Catholic Church be the Mother of Harlots? Does it order its children to commit adultery with global sovereigns? Is this an indictment of modern religion?

The Abominations of the Earth = 271

This title is derived from the Book of Daniel in a few references; maybe the most known is this one.

> Then I heard a holy one speaking; and another holy one said to that certain one who was speaking, "How long will the vision be, concerning the daily sacrifices and the transgression of desolation, the giving of both

the sanctuary and the host to be trampled under foot?"
(Daniel 8:13 NKJV)

Also, Jesus referred to the same in Matthew 24:15 NKJV: "Therefore when you see the 'abomination of desolation,' spoken of by Daniel the prophet, standing in the holy place (whoever reads, let him understand)."

This is a title of global power, the one that destroyed Jerusalem under the captaincy of Titus. John inferred this institution would be part of the structure that would bring the earth to its knees. It was an abomination because it consumed the true church and put in its place an idol. This has happened many times throughout the centuries.

In the time of the Maccabees, a few hundred years before Jesus, the contemporary ruler stopped true worship in the Jewish temple at Jerusalem and placed an idol in the temple in its stead. An idol was placed again into the Jewish temple in Jerusalem around AD 69. It caused an uprising, and a year later, the temple was destroyed. Then there is the story of France, which in 1793 abolished Christian worship and the Bible, replacing pure religion with a prostitute named the goddess of reason. A few years later, Napoleon reversed the ban, and freedom of worship was restored. I maintain this abomination was a hidden political system that continues today.

Babylon the Great = 155

This is a common used title for Babylon, possibly referring to Babylon the great city. In the context, there is the word *mystery* that is dropped from "Mystery Babylon the Great" to make the calculation. It's possible this is because once the entirety of Revelation is revealed, then Babylon the Great is no longer such a mystery.

Babylon was a great city that became a desolation. But this wasn't referring so much to that great city of old but rather to a new complex commercial system that would arise. I believe we're living in that period now.

Man or Beast?

A little breathtaking maybe; some have said that 666 is the name of a single person such as Henry Kissinger, but I am the first to say this number adds up to scriptural passages. It makes sense that the greatest trouble on earth would be identified by this code.

This union of four is the first of many I have discovered. I think there might be no limit to them. Maybe there is ambiguity in Revelation 13:18: "for it is the number of a man" has led many to believe this refers to a single person. But seven heads makes it clear it doesn't refer to just one person. I think the Darby and New International Versions provide a more literal translation: "Here is wisdom. He that has understanding let him count the number of the *beast*: for it is a man's number; and its number (is) six hundred (and) sixty-six." And "This calls for wisdom. If anyone has insight, let him calculate the number of the beast, for it is man's number. His number is 666." These two versions reveal the Beast has only "man's number" rather than being a man singular or plural.

CHAPTER NINE

THE MYTHICAL BEAST

Second Union

In this second union, everything comes together. After discovering this first pattern, I wondered if this could be for real. Is it possible to calculate the number of the Beast and the 666 system by using this letter-number system? If this has any merit, surely, this would be apparent in Revelation 13, whence it came.

This seven-headed creature in a quadripartite union looked like a leopard, had the feet of a bear, spoke with a lion's mouth, and had dragon power. These creatures were first mentioned in the book of Daniel, who saw these in a series of dreams.

> And four great beasts came up from the sea, each different from the other. The first was like a lion, and had eagle's wings. I watched till its wings were plucked off; and it was lifted up from the earth and made to stand on two feet like a man, and a man's heart was given to it. And suddenly another beast, a second, like a bear. It was raised up on one side, and had three ribs in its mouth between its teeth. And they said thus to it: "Arise, devour much flesh!"
>
> After this I looked, and there was another, like a leopard, which had on its back four wings of a bird. The beast also had four heads, and dominion was given to it. After this I saw in the night visions, and behold, a fourth beast,

dreadful and terrible, exceedingly strong. It had huge iron teeth; it was devouring, breaking in pieces, and trampling the residue with its feet. It was different from all the beasts that were before it, and it had ten horns. (Daniel 7:3–7 NKJV)

An angel told Daniel what the beasts represented. This was described a few hundred years ago by Matthew Henry. The leopard was Greece, the lion was Babylon, the bear was Media-Persia, and the last was a terrible iron beast. Though not named, this beast, which looked like a dragon, was Caesar, the leader of Rome.

The four creatures were consecutive world leaders; in contrast, the Beast in Revelation 13 was a compilation of these four autonomous powers dependent on dragon power. They were as they were in the past—global entities and governors—but joined in a united front to rule the earth collectively through their various faces but with one purpose.

Maybe there are more conspiracy theories than sheep in New Zealand; conspiracies are the hallmark of modern times as they are in Revelation 13, in which the word *deception* is used nine times; simply put, conspiracies are designed to deceive. Truthers face debunkers, Wikileaks oppose governments, free people fight with banks, commercial realities do battle with Joe Blow, and the 99 percent are opposed to the 1 percent.

Humans use humans against humans to become more-powerful humans; they are unjust to other humans who have no place to flee and no courts to protect them. Powerful humans subject weaker humans to injustice. It's no surprise the angel to the prophet added these words: "He who leads into captivity shall go into captivity; he who kills with the sword must be killed with the sword. Here is the patience and the faith of the saints" (Revelation 13:10 NKJV).

Daniel and Revelation

Maybe the world has not changed significantly in these two thousand years; Revelation 13 predicted a continuation of world rulership from the morphing of Babylon, Media-Persia, Greece, and Rome into a modern democratic dictatorship. Phooey, I'm sure. How could I ever make such a rash claim? How possibly could a democracy dictate? Below the radar, that's how. These empires of old have time on their side, and they understand the ways of man, their strong weaknesses and weak strengths. Daniel added weight to this idea that Babylon, Media-Persia, and Greece, though losing global power, would continue for a time, a season: "As for the rest of the beasts, they had their dominion taken away, yet their lives were prolonged for a season and a time" (Daniel 7:12 NKJV).

This was what John spoke of over six hundred years later. But this collaboration could not have been fulfilled in John's time nor in the centuries that followed because there hadn't been the technology to fulfill Revelation 13's claim, nor have governments collaborated until today.

The Second Union: The Mythical Beast

The calculations are harmony between books. The titles to this union are a mix of Scripture from Revelation (lion mouth, bear feet, like a leopard) and the interpretation of the four kingdoms from Daniel. The fourth was the title of the ruler of the Roman state formed in 27 BC, and although *emperor* is not the term used in Scripture, in Luke 3 and most references, the term was Caesar.

The word *emperor* is derived from the Roman *imperator*; Augustus was the first with this title in 27 BC, and he remained the emperor until Jesus came of age. Then Emperor Tiberius (Luke 3) became ruler during the period Jesus grew to be a man and entered His calling.

Here are the four unions of the mythical beast.

- Babylon: lion mouth
- Media-Persia: bear feet
- Greek: like a leopard
- Roman: emperor

These letters can be converted to numbers.

Babylon: Lion Mouth

b = 2, a = 1, b = 2, y = 25, l = 12, o = 15, n = 14, l = 12, i = 9, o = 15, n = 14, m = 13, o = 15, u = 21, t = 20, h = 8 = **198**

Media-Persia: Bear Feet

m = 13, e = 5, d = 4, i = 9, a = 1, p = 16, e = 5, r = 18, s = 19, i = 9, a = 1, b = 2, e = 5, a = 1, r = 18, f = 6, e = 5, e = 5, t = 20 = **162**

Greek like a Leopard

g = 7, r = 18, e = 5, e = 5, k = 11, l = 12, i = 9, k = 11, e = 5, a = 1, l = 12, e = 5, o = 15, p = 16, a = 1, r = 18, d = 4 : = **155**

Roman Emperor

r = 18, o = 15, m = 13, a = 1, n = 14, e = 5, m = 13, p = 16, e = 5, r = 18, o = 15, r = 18 = **151**

198 + 162 + 155 +151 = 666

Mythical Beast (Second Union) Summary:

Babylon Lion mouth	198
Media-Persia Bear feet	162
Greek like a Leopard	155
Roman Emperor	151
	666

This example shows the Beast as mythical and ruling through generations and existing before Revelation was written. Morphed from the nations of the past and the future, the Beast is intergenerational, ruling like an aged tree throughout many human generations.

Babylon was the first kingdom, having its beginnings over half a millennium before the cross. The Roman emperor was the fourth and final contemporary to the days of the New Testament, having its beginnings with Caesar Augustus twenty-four years before the birth of Jesus. "Now the beast which I saw was like a leopard, his feet were like the feet of a bear, and his mouth like the mouth of a lion. The dragon gave him his power, his throne, and great authority" (Revelation 13:2 NKJV).

Babylon Lion Mouth = 198

The lion has always been synonymous with the kingdom of Babylon that stretched back to the foundation of the nations of the early world.

Babylon lion mouth is a blend of the old and the new; Daniel shows that the lion is Babylon, and Revelation shows Babylon's principal position in the Beast is like the mouth. Therefore, the phrase "Mouth of a Lion" (Revelation 13:2) and Babylon (Daniel 7:4), the lion with four wings, is Babylon lion mouth

Babylon first arose to world domination around 600 BC. In a dream, Daniel saw Babylon change from a winged beast, a grand dictatorship, into a walking animal with a man's heart, a change to civil society. Losing its military force, the country was soon overtaken by Media-Persia.

Again, Babylon was one of the three to continue for a time and a season, and it is the one named at the end chapters of the Bible. The lion of Babylon is historically recorded as an ancient symbol dating back to the sixth century BC. I believe the reference to the mouth of a lion means that this quadripartite would speak in the voice of this ancient kingdom.

Media-Persia Bear Feet = 162

This is made up from the phrase "Feet of a Bear" (Revelation 13:2) and Media-Persia from Daniel 7:5 as a bear leaning on its side.

Media-Persia ruled the world while Daniel was in the king's palace. I have always thought this nation had a democratic ability to support many kingdoms and rule over them with skill and the strength of the sword. Revelation revealed Media-Persia's role in the Beast was to be its feet, which most likely referred to its lifestyle shining through the life of this Beast. What would that represent? That is why I have named it the mystical Beast.

Greece Like a Leopard = 155

This is made up from the phrase "like a Leopard" (Revelation 13:2) and Greece from Daniel 7:6, like a leopard with four wings. It was said that Alexander the Great was as swift as a leopard as he drove the Greek kingdom to become a world power. He was just thirty when he ruled one of the largest empires of the ancient world. Revelation revealed the new role of Greece in the Beast was to be its appearance. What was the appearance of Greece? Is it not our modern Western world?

Roman Emperor = 151

The phrase *Roman emperor* is not in the book of Daniel as were the previous three, but many would agree that the fourth Beast in Daniel 7:7 with iron teeth was the Caesar who ruled the Roman Empire.

The iron teeth represented the strength of Rome, which came to power after the collapse of the Greek kingdom. Caesar's throne was powerful and feared throughout the known world; this speaks to the likeness of the dragon, the power behind the throne.

Noted World Rulers

It is astounding how these biblical union patterns consist of these recognized world empires and add to 666. These are not fly-by-night kingdoms that collapsed into obscurity. They ruled through hundreds of years during Israel's most prominent prophetic times. Daniel foretold that three of these kingdoms would continue (Daniel 7:12). John saw these merged entities driven by a single cause—to war against Christ.

Conclusion to the First Unions

From these first patterns of four, we've seen proof that the letters in *beast* add up to 666. If the wonderful message of Jesus Christ were not vehemently resisted as it is in the real world, the powerful antitype would not be positioned exactly as Revelation 13 says it is. If this monster were not a dominant force over these last two thousand years, the world would have been easily saved in the first three hundred years by the resurrection and the relentless preaching of the good news.

Jesus Christ died for the sins of the world, rose from the dead, delivered humans once and for all from the power of death, and sent His Holy Spirit to empower those who believed in Him to preach His message to the ends of the earth. While He conquered every force of hell at the cross, the implementation of His glorious victory for the human race now rests with humans themselves. We're the weak ones in this global plan of salvation.

He foresaw all things, took our weakness into account, and raised us all the same so that in the ages to come (which is now), He could show the exceeding greatness of His power toward those who believe. But the complete advent, from the cross to His glorious return, was written in a mystery.

We believe that the exceeding greatness of His power was also poured out on the day of Pentecost along with the fire and His saving power, which was spread throughout the known world. It took a forceful counterintelligence movement to resist its fast-rising influence in every sector of the world's empires then.

Satan fought the gospel early in its conception of his beastly order. They're mythical and not actually physical entities; they're allegorical pictures of real forces, puzzles to a real-world situation hidden in mystery but now revealed by whoever chooses to receive them. Their powerful tentacles of deceit invade the minds and motives of many rulers today. The players, the children, the followers, and the servants of this megalomaniac found in these unions add up to 666.

CHAPTER TEN

THE ANTICHRIST BEAST

The Beginning and Rise of the Antichrist

The word *Antichrist* is not in Revelation, though John was the only writer of the New Testament to use the word in his epistles. It is uncertain whether the epistles of John were written before or after Revelation; however, in 1 John 2:18, it was said there had been many antichrists. They were active when Jesus was born and were those who killed the Lord. *Antichrist* comes from the Greek *antiChristos*, "against Christ." The word *anti* in Greek also means "instead of." The Antichrist is the enemy of Christ and His replacement.

John said concerning the Antichrist, "He had already been, and there are many Antichrists" (1 John 2:18 NKJV). If my letter-number system is valid, it can be used to determine who this Antichrist is. Luke 3:1–2 contains all those directly involved in and ultimately responsible for Christ's death.

> Now in the fifteenth year of the reign of **Tiberius Caesar**, **Pontius Pilate** being governor of Judea, **Herod** being **tetrarch** of Galilee, his brother Philip tetrarch of Iturea and the region of Trachonitis, and Lysanias tetrarch of Abilene, while **Annas and Caiaphas** were high priests, the word of God came to John the son of Zacharias in the wilderness. (Luke 3:1–2 NKJV) **"Emphasis added"**

Out of all these people mentioned here (the words in bold), we see four groups of people whether knowingly or unknowingly joined in a conspiracy against Jesus. Their names have been written evidence for millennia.

Tiberius Caesar was the ultimate world leader and dictator of the Jews at the time Jesus was crucified. Even the chief priests of the Jews claimed Caesar was their king.

Pontius Pilate, the governor of Judea, gave the order for Jesus to be crucified. This was possible only because he was Caesar's authority over Judea and the city of the Jews.

Herod, the tetrarch of Galilee, was the governor of Galilee and had authority over Jesus because it was said Jesus belonged to that province. Pilate sent Jesus to be judged by Herod (Luke 23), but he only tortured Him before returning Him to be judged by Pilate.

Annas and Caiaphas, the elected chief and high priest of Israel and recognized rulers over the Jews, had the power to protect Jesus, but they spoke publicly that He must die and so demanded His death. They had plotted against Jesus and had handed Him over to the Roman rulers.

Tiberius Caesar

t = 20, = 9, b = 2, e = 5, r = 18, i = 9, u = 21, s = 19, c = 3, a = 1, e = 5, s = 19, a = 1, r = 18 = **150**

Pontius Pilate

p = 16, o = 15, n = 14, t = 20, i = 9, u = 21, s = 19, p = 16, i = 9, l = 12, a = 1, t = 20, e = 5 = **177**

Caiaphas High Priests

c = 3, a = 1, i = 9, a = 1, p = 16, h = 8, a = 1, s = 19, h = 8, i = 9, g = 7, h = 8, p = 16, r = 18, i = 9, e = 5, s = 19, t = 20, s = 19 = **196**

Herod Tetrarch

h = 8, e = 5, r = 18, o = 15, d = 4, t = 20, e = 5, t = 20, r = 18, a = 1, r = 18, c = 3, h = 8 = **143**

150 + 177 + 196 + 143 = 666

Antichrist Beast (Third Union) Summary:

Tiberius Caesar,	150
Pontius Pilate	177
Caiaphas high priests	196
Herod tetrarch	143
	666

Herod Tetrarch = 143

The word *tetrarchos* in Greek means "ruler of four." Herod was ruling one province of four in Israel as designated by the Roman emperor. This Herod was the one Jesus had called a fox. He was the governor for the Roman-controlled town of Galilee; he is not to be confused with Herod the Great, his father, who had died around 4 BC. He was known as Herod Antipas and Herod the Tetrarch. In this calculation, the word *the* is not included. Without a doubt, Herod was directly responsible; he had the right to dismiss the Jewish leaders and could have stopped the crucifixion, having had the ability to do so, but he did not interfere.

Pontius Pilate = 177

Jesus' fate on that terrible day rested in Pilate's hands, but he washed them, inferring, "Let this not be on me." He cast the blame on the Jews who were gathered in a huge mob, making a noisy commotion while crying out for the murderer Barabbas to be exchanged for Jesus to keep the tradition of a prisoner released once a year.

Apparently, Pilate's wife had terrible dreams concerning Jesus and requested her husband to release this innocent man. In the *Archeological Writings of the Sanhedrin and Talmuds of the Jews*, Pilate wrote of this day and how terrified he was of being overrun by the crowd, stating it was as the "Ides of March." He had no time to call in extra guards, and he was afraid the crowd would tear the city apart. He relented and sent Jesus to His death. (Archko Volume; or the Archeological Writings of the Sanhedrim and Talmuds of the Jews. Translated by Drs. McIntosh and Twyman. Records of the Senatorial Docket Taken from the Vatican Rome. Published in Philadelphia, by Antiquarian book Company 1913)

Tiberius Caesar = 150

They chose a different Christ, Caesar, in a sense, an antichrist. Caesar or Emperor Tiberius reigned from AD 14 to 37. At that time, he was officially a god to the people, and it was permitted to worship him. The Jewish rulers said, "Caesar is our King," (John 9:15), not Jesus Christ, not the Messiah, not Jesus of Nazareth, God's only begotten Son.

Caiaphas High Priests = 264

During the time and life of Jesus, the office of high priest was controlled by a father-and-son team effectively operating as one. These two were the chief and high priests who'd prophesied the death of Jesus, who'd plotted the death of Jesus, who had compelled Pilate to judge Jesus, and who had coerced the Jews into demanding Jesus be crucified. It is no surprise that the title for this pattern of four would be "Caiaphas high priests."

This office was appointed by the Roman rulers, never by the Jewish council. Caiaphas, the son of Annas, was the official high priest answerable directly to Roman authority, but here the title is plural, "high priests," and rightly so. Annas, his father, the high and chief priest who had ruled before Caiaphas, still ruled Israel through Caiaphas. "High priests" is accurate as two were in charge, but legally, the office belonged to Caiaphas, and so it's one person but in the plural form.

Four Became One

Whether knowingly or unknowingly, these four rulers were together for one purpose. They had the power to protect Jesus or send Him to an agonizing death. All four chose the latter. These four are significant in history. None can doubt they existed and participated to some measure in the Messiah's death.

The first two union examples drawn from Scripture were allegories of how Satan operates, but this third union was a historic event. These four rulers murdered Christ without a cause. John said there had been many, and by this enigma of numbers, the start of this antichrist movement was unveiled.

Here is another configuration to this union pattern of these four, with Annas added as the same as the fourth, the high priests.

Antichrist

Herod tetrarch	143
Pontius Pilatus	212
Caesar	47
High Priests Caiaphas and Annas	264
	666

This pattern lacks something; it's not a solid result because Pilate's name Pontius Pilatus uses the Greek spelling. A truly credible union pattern would be evenly matched, conclusive, compelling, and without doubt. However, the outcome of this pattern is accurate and has all the four as the previous.

Consider back in their day if these four had been labeled antichrists. What would the reaction have been? Would they have been insulted? I don't think Jesus of Nazareth was held in such high regard or disregard. No ruler would have cared much for the biblical claims of the Messiah's kingly estate. These four involved in the death of Jesus would care little for the title Antichrist.

Did the actions of Herod Tetrarch, Pontius Pilatus, Caesar, and high priests Caiaphas and Annas make them beyond redemption? No. And you need to understand this before knowing what the contemporary unions are. Though these titles and positions are filled by humans, no matter the crime, all humans can find salvation with Christ whether they were directly involved or not with His death.

Though Caiaphas was the high priest, his father Annas had a controlling influence over the office. Even so, Caiaphas proved he was his own man by his reports to the Sanhedrin concerning the resurrection. He thoroughly investigated the many stories about Jesus' body having been taken and His raising from the dead.

Caiaphas came to the conclusion it was a true event. He resigned from his office under the conviction that the office of the high priest could no longer be functional. The full report along with other reports concerning eyewitnesses of the death of Jesus are in *The Archaeological Writings of the Sanhedrin and Talmud of the Jews*, translated into English a few hundred years ago by McIntosh and Twyman. (Archko Volume; or the Archeological Writings of the Sanhedrim and Talmuds of the Jews. Translated by Drs. McIntosh and Twyman. Records of the Senatorial

Docket Taken from the Vatican Rome. Published in Philadelphia, by Antiquarian book Company 1913)

The last biblical mention of Caiaphas is in Acts 4, at the questioning of the apostles by the Sanhedrin. They were asking as to what manner they performed miracles. If Caiaphas believed the reports of the resurrection, it is possible he could have been converted. This is terrific news. He had been involved in the worst crime of all since the fall. Yet this crime was predestined to become a great story about mercy and the redeeming power of the resurrection and the life of Jesus Christ, the Son of God, who can save all people.

The Rise of Unseen Kingdoms

If there were truly a predestined time of salvation given to the earth (I mean that ironically), if truly this were that time, Jesus came and conquered the world of darkness in one blinding event as Scriptures relate. If this were the day that all the forces of hell fell, it was for just for a moment; they speedily reorganized themselves. When Jesus came forth from the tomb, hell was in retreat, but when Jesus ascended to heaven, maybe all Satan's powers saw a great opportunity.

At that time, the rulers of darkness quickly restructured their global organizations and changed their strategies. These have continued to change, and the earth became a battlefield for truth and freedom.

The roots of the changes instituted by the powers of darkness can be understood in the administration of Jesus' incarceration; after Herod mocked Jesus in his palace, he returned Him to Pilate, and they became the best of buddies: "That very day Pilate and Herod became friends with each other, for previously they had been at enmity with each other" (Luke 23:12 NKJV). This was the beginning of the unification of the kingdoms of darkness; they were drawn together for a single purpose; Satan had structured a plan to destroy this crowning victory at the cross.

From the time of the resurrection, around AD 30–33, and throughout the coming ages, the kingdoms of the earth have been molded by such incredible change that the name and life of Jesus became the most prominent issue in European society even a thousand years after His resurrection. Exactly how this could have happened is a historical mystery.

A thousand years later, the name of Jesus hadn't faded into oblivion; around 1000 AD, all Europe was turned upside down by the teachings of the priests that Jesus was soon to return. All of Europe feared the teachings and responded to them in any way they knew. The kings themselves publicly accepted the ideas and did benevolent works to show themselves to their people that they weren't antichrists. The battle to wipe out the true Christian faith since AD 30 has led only to failure. The battle still rages, but the forces of evil work more to usurp and mimic.

Throughout these generations, this beast union has continued its tyranny on earth to destroy freedom and reign sovereign over all flesh. Scripture reveals the real cause of the action against Christians, the fighting, the resisting, the usurpation, and the mimicking. This organized power has ruled for generations. It still aims to root out and destroy all truth and those who call upon the name of the Lord.

Although he'd like to declare, "Resistance is futile," Satan's dominion and victory isn't idyllic or sweet. At the other side of the battle for our minds and lives is God, whose eyes burn with fire. His garments are as white and dazzling as the sun. He is dripping in the blood of the redemption that He championed for humanity. He is mighty, merciful, and victorious. No one in heaven, on earth, or under the earth can contend against Him and His mighty name.

Chapter Eleven

THE BEAST OF INFORMATION

Decoding the Beast

The Beast is described as a mythological animal that controls the earth. Revelation appears to be madness and fantasy until the writer challenges us with a riddle: we can know this Beast by a number, the number of man, 666.

Numbers are used to develop programming languages, the basis of the Internet, which has enveloped social and commercial entities. So here we have a mythological animal represented by real numbers based on a coding system. It was assembled from four parts: lion, leopard, bear, and dragon, so logically, the number 666 also comprises four parts.

I am particularly fond of this first contemporary union. As it is in the computer world, everything is so connected; a multiplicity of systems within systems, partnerships, companies, various hardware, and multiple codes attempt to work together and deliver data, knowledge, information, and clarity but also control, command, and mega profits.

Beasts of Information

Computer

c = 3, o = 15, m = 13, p = 16, u = 21, t = 20, e = 5, r = 18 = **111**

Internet

i = 9, n = 14, t = 20, e = 5, r = 18, n = 14, e = 5, t = 20 = **105**

International Business Machines

i = 9, n = 14, t = 20, e = 5, r = 18, n = 14, a = 1, t = 20, i = 9, o = 15, n = 14, a = 1, l = 12, b = 2, u = 21, s = 19, i = 9, n = 14, e = 5, s = 19, s = 19, m = 13, a = 1, c = 3, h = 8, i = 9, n = 14, e = 5, s = 19 = **332**

Microsoft

m = 13, i = 9, c = 3, r = 18, o = 15, s = 19, o = 15, f = 6, t = 20 = **118**

Beast of Information

Computer	111
International Business Machines	332
Microsoft	118
Internet	105
	666

Summary Beast of Information

For every member of a body to work together, each needs to communicate with the others or the whole body will not function. These four entities established standards for collaborative communication that are at the foundation of computing. Very possibly, without IBM and Microsoft, computing and the Internet as we know them today would never have evolved.

IBM became the representative of the universal type of hardware configuration that became the standard for all desktop computing. Microsoft represents the software standards that became the universal configuration of every desktop computer, and every competing application eventually adopted Microsoft standards. Without these, the Internet wouldn't have flourished; with them, the concept of systems talking to systems proliferated worldwide.

Computer = 111

Here is another wonderful microscopic enigma. Why would a computer, which relies on binary code, have the numerical value of a binary code, 111. The binary system is based solely on the numbers 1 and 0. The number 111 in this system equals 7, a perfect prime, and although it all might mean nothing, I don't think it's just a matter of chance the free-world gamblers like to assume. Another couple of prominent names add up to 111: *New York* and *sorceries*. Is that not crazy?

What gave computing its legs was the development of silicon-based electronics in the early seventies. But even before this, punch-card computing was popular in industries needing calculating power. This technology dates back to the eighteenth century and was used in the textile industry.

International Business Machines = 332

IBM was a company that most likely began with punch-card technology. IBM archives reveal that by 1937, thirty-two presses were providing 10 million punched cards per day. No surprise that conspiracies are rife about the company's efforts in providing logistics for the war effort.

During the sixties, magnetic tapes were used for data storage, and when computing technology exceeded mainframe capabilities, IBM was at the forefront of the industry, its sunrise developer. It set hardware standards that came to fruition around the early eighties.

The most memorable was the first—the IBM Personal Computer XT, which relied on a DOS (disk operation system); computers could then handle many tasks besides word processing.

Microsoft = 118

The only word I found that had the same numerical value of *Microsoft* was *Guy Fawkes*. Well, how could we not all agree that this software went off with a bang and garnered global recognition in under a decade? The dawn of modern computing began with wedding bells; IBM and Microsoft partnered as the blue giants and decided to leave code development to others. This opened a great door of opportunity for Gates and partners.

With the vision of a personal computer in every household, they developed the first DOS code, and through time, mergers, hacks, integration, acquisitions, and hundreds of thousands of programming hours, Microsoft managed to become the industry standard, the most-used desktop platform in the world and by default the system style every other desktop operation system needed to conform to.

I need to say here that just because I consider these entities components of the Beast system, that doesn't muddy the moral fabric of those involved. Gates, one of the richest people in the world, uses his wealth to help developing nations, as do other tech billionaires. Their hearts might be in the right place, but that doesn't mean this beastly scenario can be avoided.

Internet = 105

The Internet is the unseen power of the other three. While the mouth of the Beast would maybe be the computer, the appearance Microsoft, and the feet, its basis, IBM, the Internet is totally dependent on these three; without them, it would be just another Jules Verne fantasy.

These four technology entities act as one; through these four, global control has begun to be realized. The Internet gives the power to the innocent, who give the information, and the guilty, who misuse that information. It is not mere coincidence that this adds up to 666. These are words that have not been manipulated; nothing has been added to or taken away from them to force the calculation. It has the purity of the first union, the Beast of Babylon.

Beast of Data

United States Department of Defense	352	USDoD
PRISM	75	
Internet	105	
Software Code	134	
	666	

Within this global information monster is the ability to control liberty beyond acceptable human boundaries. Data mining is a modern buzzword for organizations requiring any form of public or private information. More than just collecting, the miner uses tools on large data packages, called big data, to analyze information trends and patterns.

United States Department of Defense = 352

The CIA and the U.S. Department of Defense began to work more in harmony apparently after 9/11, after a select committee reviewed their activities. Interestingly, they have seven departments represented by seven emblems. This is a very large organization with big money to protect the interests of the United States.

Prism = 75

PRISM is the brainchild of the CIA; it is a clandestine, mass, electronic surveillance system launched by the NSA in 2007.

Internet = 105

Well, I've written enough about the Internet already, but it is an unseen power hidden behind the throne. Certainly, the entire world has become dependent on this unseen, virtual, interactive knowledge bank.

Software Code = 134

At first, I thought *software* and *code* were a little ambiguous; aren't they the same? Maybe not. There are software applications and code that is not an application. Software refers to the entire makeup of any programs that run computers whereas code are better understood as the individual lines of programs. In any case, there can be no doubt that these four are connected in the entity called NSA for the collection of data.

The most targeted information is in regard to the security of the nation, and for the most part, honest Americans need to be thankful these tools are at their disposal. Could this configuration of powers be used for more than just national protection? Absolutely. And at the end of the day, who can stop any wayward activities?

The Young Ones

The methods of collecting personal or private information is very young; unlike as is the case in movies, not everything is being monitored in real time. The current system focuses predominately on commerce, and all the systems work best when revenue is the reward. Though even in commerce, not all things are bound by this system because greenbacks aren't. Just how long paper notes will continue is difficult to predict, but currently, cash is still king. Many other methods of communication and information transfer are free from snooping, including handwritten or typed letters, possibly the best encryption system sent by good ol' snail mail.

Talks in the countryside are out of reach of listening devises, that is, if you've left your iPhone at home. Also, there are many security tricks you can put to use that are on the Internet if indeed you're troubled by all this. Remember that Snowden was just one of the many operatives in the system. What he perceived and believed had been affected by their conditioning of him for the task he was doing; he was just a pawn in that operation, not a leader, a developer, or a director. He knew only what others had told him.

The Internet is undergoing change just as peoples, nations, and organizations are, but conformity is gaining ground. The Internet's chief architects are developing plans to bring it out of the closet to make their mass-surveillance needs appear acceptable to the populace.

Snow saw this immaturity in his quote #2: "I believe that at this point in history, the greatest danger to our freedom and way of life comes from the reasonable fear of omniscient State powers kept in check by nothing more than policy documents." (27 Edward Snowden Quotes About U.S. Government Spying That Should Send A Chill Up Your Spine

By Michael Snyder, on June 10th, 2013)

I believe there's enough power in the hands of global e-manipulators to bring nations to their knees and crying out for an acceptable level of e-personal slavery to be mandated for society. If the power of a dragon is driving it, human efforts to resist will be tossed aside. "Resistance is futile," declared the Borg.

The concept of technology dates from the previous century, but the concept of data mining goes back only six years or so. It's face is changing; it is becoming visible, and soon, it will become acceptable, trusted, and popular.

The architects will be able to do this because systems of control have become socially acceptable over the years. Don't get me wrong here; there are many opponents, voices, leakers, anons, the shocked, and the politicizing who are working against this, but even the strongest freedom movements could appear to be just marketing voices trying to normalize the situation.

The new frontiers' that struggle against the powers that add up to 666.

Copyright Beast

Dotcom Megaupload = 165

There is no short story on Kim Dotcom, who owned one of the largest community file-sharing websites, Megaupload. He made hundreds of millions, was targeted by the copyright holders, and the powers to be that collect taxes from the owners of the data have challenged his overnight success. He's currently incarcerated in a multimillion-dollar mansion just outside Auckland City. Is he a voice of freedom or a development tool for the implementation of international copyright laws?

Julian Assange Wikileaks = 233

From the copyright battles in New Zealand, we go across the ditch to a very serious Australian involved in this new electronic freedom movement. Assange began the website Wikileaks around 2010, mixing his programming and journalism skills. He is now embattled in transboundary politics as he claims the United States wants to lock him up. Like Kim, he's restricted to the embassy of Ecuador in London, and also like Kim, he has helped give eyes to a blind world and ready them for future they'll all have little control over.

Senate Bill 968 = 122

Senate Bill 968 I believe is the descriptive document on the legislation of great powers to protect intellectual property and copyrights.

Protect IP Act = 146

Senate Bill 968 has the official title of "Protect IP Act"; its long title is "Preventing Real Online Threats to Economic Creativity and Theft of Intellectual Property Act of 2011." Apparently, this bill is supported by copyright and trademark owners. Well, I'm not saying this is wrong, but it's inevitable, and it's perhaps another brick in the wall that is surrounding us all.

The Drone Beast

Edward Snowden	149
National Security Agency	261
Barack Hussein Obama II	181
Drones	75
	666

Another alarming area taking us all by surprise is the newfound ability to fly stealth operations anywhere in the world and not just for data collection. Large, military-scale operations have been launched via drones to eradicate dangers with deadly weapons, and they are controlled by kids who love to play online war games. It's almost a perfect killing machine.

Edward Snowden = 149

He is the most prominent whistle-blower because of the quantity and quality of information he made available to media outlets as a contractor with in the National Security Agency organizations. In another one of those odd associations, the name *Edward Snowden* has the same numerical value as does *Judas Iscariot*. Maybe he is embarking on a similar endeavor, or maybe he is just another one involved in the market awareness campaign of the world's most powerful nation.

National Security Agency = 261

The National Security Agency is an American intelligence organization involved with collecting and mining global data. This is a post–World War II agency formed by Truman in 1952, but its origins date back to 1917. There is controversial information claiming that the NSA gathers information to formulate targets for drones.

Barack Hussein Obama II = 181

It's claimed that before he was elected, Obama promised to reduce the number of drone attacks, but the kills have exceeded the number of kills during the Bush administration by a factor of ten.

Drones = 75

Drones are either unmanned vehicles used for surveillance or combat vehicles used in military operations. They range in size, and they are either planes or quadcopters. I can't think of anything that currently matches the fifth and sixth trumpets of Revelation as well as do these drones. They strike fear into people's hearts; these horrific war machines can strike without warning. What will happen in fifty years when all nations have them?

In summary, we've seen how various contemporary organizations join in calculating to 666. They're technology based, government based, industry based, and commercially successful. They're young and developing; they have unknown future potentialities. Today, the impossible is becoming possible; technological miracles are common, but the poor get poorer while the rich become richer. Everything has changed but nothing has changed. What will the end be?

CHAPTER TWELVE

THE FUTURE BEAST

Here's my prediction about how technology fits into the 666 enigma. All computers have Internet connections or gateways identified as IP addresses, Internet protocol addresses, unique numbers assigned to every device operating on the Internet.

In the future, these IP addresses could run every major device from planes and handhelds to cars, household appliances, and drones, and they could even be in wristbands to track children and pets. Currently, the governing bodies are neutral entities, simple registries for the purpose of the Internet. But this could change; IP addresses could be controlled by bureaus subordinate to a single global bureau for the purposes of control.

The Signposts

There could be various reasons for such control; the bureaus would have rules for objectives to be realized. Any entity varying from the rules could have its IP usage disconnected or hindered.

The ultimate signposts to this system eventuating could be the development of, say, a multilateral, contractual joining of sovereign entities. We are already seeing global heavyweights interfering with those nations who seek autonomy. As technology becomes a greater enabler of systems of control, the NSA and the CIA could become global enforcers. It just seems too easy.

Christianity came on to the world stage in a mighty clash with world powers. Caesar and his allies fought against the new moral movement until they finally joined ranks with it around the year 300 and assimilated the purity of Christian dogma. From then on, the beloved "oil" of the movement dissipated and Christianity became nothing but a theological and political institution.

Centuries passed, and then as Isaiah had foreseen, from the seeds of righteousness came again a hunger for truth. This in turn birthed a renewal, and in time, the true operation of the Christian movement was again building among the hearts and lives of humans: "Their descendants shall be known among the Gentiles, and their offspring among the people. All who see them shall acknowledge them, that they are the posterity whom the LORD has blessed" (Isaiah 61:9 NKJV).

If Caesar had the power of the Internet, our freedom would have been long since lost. We'd no longer have freedom of choice, particularly about salvation and the Christian life. However, God's ultimate plan is coming to fullness as the tools of electronic accountability have begun to arrive passively on earth.

There is a force of nature, something in an unseen realm, that is pushing the world to absolute bondage and slavery, and it's possibly controlled by a small, elite group. The current setbacks they have faced due to recent disclosures are possibly only minor. So many movies in the last fifty years have been about the dangers of global control through technology, but I'm afraid they have proven simply to normalize the inevitable. My friends, when you remove all the fine apparel of every cause and movement, I predict you'll find they are all social engineering experiments aimed at reducing or eradicating our freedoms, but that idea lacks the essential evidence that well-funded research requires. These predictions are being normalized; TV programs such as *Person of Interest* almost brag about the inevitable; fiction rules modern thinking and in so doing suffocates truth; it makes the surreal believable.

When all the infrastructure of the Internet is in place, will we risk losing all our freedoms? What will force the issue? A few small global disasters followed by a calamity? That's the logical approach governments will take to implementing a system that will save us all. Is that day fast approaching? Has not the groundwork been laid? We wait for the masterstroke to complete its magnificence.

Seven Simple Steps for World Control

Here are seven simple steps we can take to change the world. Keep in mind that the rollout of IP-driven technology such as handhelds is still on a pathway to maturity. It could be years before all nations have the infrastructure and the skills to implement it, but that doesn't change the madness; it only delays it.

1. Personnel files would be compiled for every human and entity and include information such as IP addresses, mobile phone numbers, tax numbers, locations, nationalities, trading habits, purchases, health, life expectancy, consumption, genealogy, metadata, connections, debt, vocations, religion, sports, global and local usefulness, intelligence, and achievements.

2. Multilateral agreements would combine global management of personal files and collection and include IP address allocations; mandates would be implemented for every device and transaction to be solely implemented through an IP address.

3. Personnel files would be globally managed by a newly formed organization called the IP Address Bureau. The files would be renamed "Citizen Data" and "Entity Data" and become integrated in technology changes. IP addresses would be issued globally through the bureau as specific number for all things and replace all previous numbers including tax numbers; they can be then like personal phone numbers.

4. World Bank would introduce credit ratios for Citizen Data and Entity Data rankings.

5. United Nations would introduce a moral policy that affects Citizen Data and Entity Data rankings.

6. All multilateral organizations would sign "Cashless" pacts; all trading would be solely through the Internet, and credit wouldbe issued according to Citizen Data and Entity Data rankings.

7. You're left with a choice—believe what they tell you to believe to increase your Citizen Data and Entity Data rankings or fight this and endanger your credit rating to trade and even risk having your IP address disabled and be no longer able to buy anything.

Inevitable Beast

Here are some possible Future IP Unions.

Internet Protocol	219
World Bank	100
United Nations	165
Rothschild Family	182
	666

These four all exist and reveal a possible future collaboration between the ability to connect through the Internet and global organizations that could use the connection to control the user.

Internet Protocol = 219

IP addresses to connect to the Internet are unique; every device requires an IP address. Most commonly, these numbers are constructed of sets of four digits. If you type "IP address" into Google search, it will reply with your IP address. This is a simplistic description of a complex system. However, the point is that this protocol is global and enables millions of devices to work interactively.

World Bank = 100

We all know the World Bank, founded 1944, and its spread throughout the world as its title says.

United Nations = 165

The United Nations works closely with the World Bank. These organizations with their strong political backbone keep themselves away from controversy; as do all political institutions, they do most their work behind the scenes.

Rothschild Family = 182

This is the most famous banking family that has been the subject of more conspiracy theories about its plans for world dominion than its members would ever care for. They are almost reclusive. I think it would surprise no one to see the family on the same list as the World Bank and United Nations, but there has never been much connection between them and the Internet, so this can be another one to add to their conspiracy list.

E-trade Beast: The Fictitious Future

I believe at some time in world affairs, we'll see that perfect union rising up out of the earth, water, and ashes of intergovernmental organizations, multinational corporations, technologies, and commerce. I'm not sure when this will happen; I'm just laying claim to the idea that the groundwork is already in place, the writing already on the wall, and the warnings already in our daily marketplace. This next, the e-trade beast is a fictitious example of these future possibilities.

E-trade Beast

WWW	69
IP Address Bureau	163
World Trade Organization	269
United Nations	165
	666

Certainly, this scenario would be a perfect blend of global institutions and technology, but it is only hypothetical, not a prediction. We should keep our eyes open for this; some time, these crazy things will happen.

WWW = 69

The acronym WWW for World Wide Web and the beginning letters in website addresses has become the code that runs the Internet based on hypertext. This was invented around 1989 by an ex-CERN employer and used to help share research.

IP Address Bureau = 163

Out of these four, the IP address bureau is fictitious but a possibility. Something will become the global kingmaker, and it could use this title.

World Trade Organization = 269

WTO is a multilateral institution that came out of the General Agreement on Tariffs and Trade, a postwar organization formed to promote international economic cooperation with the Bretton Woods institutions, the World Bank and the International Monetary Fund.

United Nations = 165

This is possibly the greatest of all multilateral organizations and the mother of many others.

CHAPTER THIRTEEN

THE CONSPIRACY BEAST

Decoding Today's Conspiracies

As the world is rife with conspiracy theories, I thought to test some of these against the 666 quad union model. If there's any fire among the smoke, there would also be some beastly examples. A couple of currently hot topics reveal just that, and the greatest of these involve aviation incidents.

The Beasts of 9/11

We all awoke in September 2001 to a different world after the disaster that befell the World Trade Center in New York. That day, Western nations shut down in shock and horror. A Google search for "September Eleven" results in more than 133 million hits. Many conspiracy theories have been voiced about 9/11, so here are a few more.

I have researched religious and terrorist organizations, and we know that the perpetrators have died, but have the instigators been caught? I think the idea of it being an inside job is to damning for anyone to comprehend. I would prefer to see the blame pass on to the one really to blame—the Beast that has been manipulating the earth for centuries.

Patriot Beast

World Trade Center	185
September eleven	166
PATRIOT Act	123
e pluribus unum	192
	666

World Trade Center = 185

Most of the buildings belonging to the World Trade Center were brought down during the 9/11 attack. The world was watching in shock as planes flew into the twin towers.

September Eleven = 166

Long version of 9/11, inferring the date 9.11.01

Patriot Act = 123

If there was a conspiracy here, it was a hidden agenda. Just two weeks after that the terrible event of 9/11, President Bush signed the Patriot Act, which I believe could be the foundational document for current NSA operations.

e pluribus unum = 192

E pluribus unum is a motto on the great seal of the United States.

World Trade Center Beast

The World Trade Center has seven buildings all of which fell on that terrible day. Just as there are yearly remembrances for the ending of World War II, so there will forever be remembrances of this catastrophic day. These seven towers had individual names; the buildings that were destroyed in the terrorist attack and the new buildings that are replacing them are named WTC 1 to WTC 7.

World Trade Center Beast strays outside the quad union, but it's interesting all the same. I have taken the old names and added them up with interesting results.

World Trade Center Beast

7 World Trade Center	192	7 WTC
U.S. Customs House	218	6 WTC
130 Liberty Street,	182	5 WTC
150 Greenwich Street	185	4 WTC
Vista International	223	3 WTC
World Trade Center	185	2 WTC
Freedom Tower	147	1 WTC
2x 666	**1332**	

These old buildings being rebuilt on their historical sites calculate to 1,332, two times 666, two generations of 666. Is this the wound that was healed? Does this show the two lives of the 666 system? Does this mean the new World Trade Towers will be the new Babylon? Will they partition off Manhattan and form a new sovereign nation like the Vatican? That's a page we should keep watching.

7 World Trade Center = 192

WTC 7 was originally forty-two stories high and was damaged by the attacks of September 11. The new building is fifty-seven stories tall and was completed in 2006.

U.S. Customs House = 218

WTC 6, on the One World Trade Center site, has been demolished for a World Trade Center and September 11 Memorial and Museum.

130 Liberty Street = 182

WTC 5, like buildings 6 and 7, suffered structure damage and was demolished. Negotiations are still underway for its successor.

150 Greenwich Street = 185

WTC 4, originally a nine-story building, was damaged beyond repair after the attacks. The new high-rise of seventy-two floors opened in 2013.

Vista International = 223

WTC 3, a twenty-two-story World Trade Center hotel, was damaged by airplane landing gear falling on its roof. The replacement is an eighty-floor high-rise to be completed in 2017.

World Trade Center = 185

WTC 2, one of the twins, the South Tower, was seventy-nine stories and towered over Manhattan. It came crashing down on that terrible day. A seventy-nine-floor replacement is planned to be completed in 2020.

Freedom Tower = 147

WTC 1, the other twin, dubbed the Freedom Tower, also known as One World Trade Center, was also seventy-nine stories and I think a copy of WTC 2. Both towers were destroyed by the planes. This site has been crowned with a superstructure, the tallest in America, 526 meters and 104 floors. This was just opened at the end of 2014.

9/11 Beast

In this mini spreadsheet regarding 9/11, there are three numbers that add to 666. Not four this time, but I just thought it was interesting, as there was four planes involved and their flight numbers total 356. By adding this number to the two building centers these planes crashed into, World Trade Center and the Pentagon, they add up to 666. I mean really, isn't that the strangest of things?

9/11 Beast

11+175+77+93	**356**	*Aviation Disaster Flight Numbers*
World Trade Center	185	
The Pentagon	125	
	666	

Flights, 11 + 175 + 77 + 93 = 356

- **Flight 11:** American Airlines flight 11 crashed into the North Tower with ninety-two people onboard.
- **Flight 175:** United Airlines flight 175 crashed into the South Tower with sixty-five people onboard.
- **Flight 77:** American Airlines flight 77 crashed into the Pentagon with sixty-four people onboard.
- **Flight 93:** United Airlines flight 93 crashed in Somerset County, Pennsylvania, with forty-four people onboard. This plane was thought to be en route to the White House but was stopped by brave passengers.

World Trade Center = 185

These are the twin towers that flights 175 and 11 crashed into, causing over three thousand deaths.

The Pentagon = 125

This is the American military building flight 77 crashed into. It's the headquarters of the U.S. Department of Defense. Note the use of the word "the," which is the official title.

Aviation Mysteries

Another aviation mystery concerns plane disasters. Flight 370, the Malaysian Boeing 777, disappeared from radar after ninety minutes of flight. There is no information about what exactly happened to this flight with 239 people onboard.

Flight QZ8501 was caught a storm in December 2014; unexpected turbulence caused the plane to crash. The wreckage was found in the sea.

Flight MH17 was a war fatality; it was shot down by a missile over Ukraine.

In the latter two calamities, bodies were recovered, black boxes were found, investigations were carried out, and reports were complete. This, however, has not been the case with flight 370.

Mystery Flight 370

Flight 370 (62 + 370)	432	
USDoD	63	United States Department of Defense
WTC	46	World Trade Center
The Pentagon	125	
	666	

Flight 370

The crash of this flight remains a mystery; it has no convincing explanation. The Malaysian opposition leader claimed a cover-up, and new articles suggested foul play. This is because the plane had a near-perfect record and was considered to be the best of the best. It was an aircraft that utilized cutting-edge technology. Could it have flown unmanned? Could the controls have been taken over? While I think the answer is yes, I believe it wouldn't be that easy. They're not generic systems as seen in movies—just plug in the notebook and start banging on the keys. It was a sophisticated aircraft with many built-in, fail-safe features.

Many in-house people would have had to have remained silent for this to have been a simple case of theft. This event highlights gaps in global monitoring, which all nations will have to engage in.

PART 3

CHAPTER FOURTEEN

LIVING IN THE DAY

Today's Beast: Revelation 13

It is very simple to identify many organizations that could be part of the Beast, so we have to determine what exactly the Beast in Revelation 13 is. We've described its physical and virtual attributes, but we have to understand that it is a global entity. The following seven attributes will help us determine if any entity is affiliated with it.

Seven Scriptural Attributes of the Beast

1. Was wounded but healed: "And I saw one of his heads as if it had been mortally wounded, and his deadly wound was healed" (Revelation 13:3 NKJV). Isn't it wonderful when the hero suffers great setbacks including near-death experiences? I can think of a few great religions whose founders suffered the same. This shows us also that the organized invasion suffered setbacks that worked out to its advantage.

   What exactly these setbacks are is opinion and conjecture, just like the rest of this book, so here it goes. Every marauding onslaught has been met with a justifiable countermeasure, so the Beast's plan of world domination has suffered many defeats. But a new plan comes after every defeat; the Beast is not conquered.

2. **He is marveled upon**: "And all the world marveled and followed the beast" (Revelation 13:3 NKJV). Navel-gazing is a common trend,

one adopted more so by the young, emotionally undernourished nations that look at America with great admiration.

This goes much deeper. The Greek *theaomai* means "to look closely at." In my opinion, this comes from drug-induced encounters. Drugs are the largest cause of phobias, though again it's all conjecture. But here is the birth of religion versus the birth of the Christian movement. Jesus never gave Himself over to any type of strong alcohol or drugs and remained coherent on the cross. In His time of greatest agony, He refused medication. Years later, there rose three great religions all birthed on battlefields. In the ancient times of battle, strong alcohol or opiate-based medications were used without modern concepts of ideal dosages. The wounded were mostly overmedicated and thus hallucinated. The fantasy worlds they entered were confused with reality.

So it is my opinion that the three proceeding religious movements were founded on opiate-based hallucinations. This becomes then a marveling upon people who aren't thinking right; they want to put people on great pedestals and even place themselves on the same; their pride and arrogance erodes moral reality, and soon they'll do anything for that feeling of supremacy.

3. **Feared in war:** "Who is like the beast? Who is able to make war with him?" (Revelation 13:4 NKJV). In this world, there is some you don't muck with. All nations feared the Beast.

4. **Worshipped**: "So they worshiped the dragon who gave authority to the beast; and they worshiped the beast" (Revelation 13:4 NKJV). People can worship something they can't see; they've been doing that for millennia. To see this, one needs to hop off planet earth for a while and question the reasons behind the world's activities. You'll see it when you can't answer the reasons for things that are well supported in society and among all nations such as patriotism, acceptable inequality, and religion with no reality.

5. **Has Limited Power over the Saints**: "Make war with the saints" (Revelation 13:7 NKJV). I say limited because in the previous

chapter, "they overcame him by," but here, it's overcoming the saints. *Overcome* is used for victory over the Beast and Satan's power, but in this context, the saints are being subdued. This is a fact, for many centuries of Christian failure and defeat have been recorded. Modern talk of the victorious Christian is all of thirty years old as opposed to over nineteen hundreds years of this gritty faith that suffered loss, death, sickness, and poverty for the faith. "And they overcame him by the blood of the Lamb and by the word of their testimony, and they did not love their lives to the death" (Revelation 12:11 NKJV). Rather, "It was granted to him to make war with the saints and to overcome them" (Revelation 13:7 NKJV).

Is not a promise of hope but a real picture of real-world events. It doesn't take away from any promise. The power is limited; the choice is up to the individual saints to accept God's sovereign plan of protection, health, and prosperity. It's up to them; nobody can force them, and when they do find the truth, they will find there is a battle to withhold the truth. This confirms the real picture of Revelation 13:7. Satan has no power over those whose names appear in the Book of Life and thus has limited power.

6. **Practices deception:** "And he deceives those who dwell on the earth" (Revelation 13:14 NKJV). Conspiracy theories pop up more and more. Many governments specialize in various deceptive measures. The deception industry has its market leaders who make it socially acceptable.

7. **Has total global authority:** "And he exercises all the authority of the first beast in his presence, and causes the earth and those who dwell in it to worship the first beast, whose deadly wound was healed" (Revelation 13:12 NKJV). I believe this authority is more active in the entity of the four joined together while it's assumed each of the four also has a global mandate. There are in these last days many global entities that work to secure the rewards with every tool at their disposal.

What Could Be Done Right Now?

- Sovereign countries could consider security and data policies to be autonomous and local data as sovereign.
- Laws could institute longevity to paper copies and public access to paper copies.
- Off-line data bank systems could be created and wrapped in sovereign law of that nation.
- Copyright could be developed to outright own a national language and heritage.
- Everyone should be careful about the powers these entities have. Most data reduces to a text format. The original form of basic computer systems never needed to be online. All that was generated for software publishers to help control their assets, the software code you're using. A computer could easily keep information safe and private for decades by being off-line. This would be more beneficial than the modern push to the cloud.
- Everything can have a paper backup though that would be time consuming. But it was only a few years ago that we relied on snail mail rather than email. Quite the revolution, but should we lose our grassroots habits?
- Every person should take responsibility for his or her personal information, and it should be in paper form.
- Should NSA and sovereign America disclose the nations they have spied on? No one wants to think America is the Antichrist, but its global data collection capability is worrisome. What controls should be put on the United States and the European community? Have they gone too far? What controls should be put in place to ensure sovereignty?

It's about Your Children

You could ask, "Who cares?" because you might think this is all twenty years away and you can worry about it then. But when that day comes crashing, you'll have only a few avenues of escape and will hope there is a God who will save you. When the world reaches the point that synthetic perfection is preferred over life itself and noncompliance is punishable by death, it will be too late for your children, who will be caught in a web with no escape.

If evil forces haven't cleansed the world of everything not conducive to a same-gender world, God help us if we cannot find a Bible. If libraries are destroyed, the whole world will communicate online. A publisher could update and change the truth, change history, change Bible translations, and change all manner of habits and choices by simply copying and pasting.

Resist the Beast

Here are some examples of Scripture that explicitly uncover Satan's strategies: "It was granted to him to make war with the saints and to overcome them. And authority was given him over every tribe, tongue, and nation" (Revelation 13:7 NKJV). "Then he opened his mouth in blasphemy against God, to blaspheme His name, His tabernacle, and those who dwell in heaven" (Revelation 13:6 NKJV).

Though it never says what the blasphemies were, I think they were a legal strategy to obtain an injunction against the work of the cross and the witnesses of that work in the earth. If a billionaire leaves his estate to his butler, his descendants might file an injunction against the estate and freeze its assets until legal action is settled. Likewise, Satan was for a long time trying to nullify the victory of the saints in Christ.

These same concepts are shown throughout Revelation. I believe the Beast's accusations are in retaliation to the legal work of the cross. Maybe this could have been the basis of the battle for these few thousand years, and if this were the case, we need to give more merit to instruction on faith.

Usurp and Mimic Counterfeit Christianity

I suggest the most effectual part of Satan's plan is his attempt to cause confusion among the unbelievers. Satan has a strategic plan to hinder and subvert the truth of Christianity. This operation is not exterior to the Christian Church but is alive and active within and without. Here is where most of the confusion lies.

"Then I saw another beast coming up out of the earth, and he had two horns like a lamb and spoke like a dragon" (Revelation 13:11 NKJV). This second beast has two horns like a lamb; I believe its description is that of a countermovement, a counterfeit Christianity. Religious organizations try to appear the same, but they are in every way different from the real Christian movement. They are not to be confused, though, with the many good churches in the world; these counterfeit movements are for the most part organizations ordained and promoted by governments.

> He performs great signs, so that he even makes fire come down from heaven on the earth in the sight of men. And he deceives those who dwell on the earth by those signs which he was granted to do in the sight of the beast, telling those who dwell on earth to make an image to the beast who was wounded by the sword and lived. (Revelation 13:13–14 NKJV)

Imposter movements dupe those who have never taken the time to understand the reality of a vibrant relationship with the Father. Those in such a relationship can't be deceived easily. I don't believe the Beast with two horns is in any way a picture of a true Christian movement that preaches the gospel and leads people to salvation through the public confession of Jesus Christ as Lord.

Seeing Babylon through the Cloud

This counterfeit movement is very effectual; it can replicate miracles and by these great signs deceive nonbelievers. I am not sure what these miracles are and what the healed wound is, but these entities have been living for generations through the organizations of priests, rulers, princes, and kings. That there is an unseen but measurable connection is unveiled by the number 666.

The Beast plans to counterfeit everything the body of Jesus Christ is called to achieve. It is rising in many types of organizations, activities, governments, intergovernmental organizations, educational organizations, research institutes, and science and technology organizations that all seem innocent but are irresponsible collectives that promote cross-cultural momentum. No one sees where it's all coming from, so it's supposed to be a normal social process. In a sense, it's organized chaos, Babylon.

The Big Picture

The Beast of Babylon is all about smoke screens and confusion. What we see is not always what is real. We don't see the power behind the throne. Smoke screens, smoking guns, deceit, rumors, false testimonies, myths, and conspiracy theories all run deep throughout society. And hey, I'm mostly likely adding to this cause.

Have you ever stood back and looked at the greater picture? Life is increasingly interconnected and complex. Corporations spend millions on branding and intellectual property; governments likewise do the same. They're working on a collective plan. Border laws are more difficult, social laws are more complex, and company laws are more complex. Some countries are becoming so bound up in red tape that the advancement of its people is being brought to a standstill through their own compliance difficulties.

Increasingly, the requirements of conformity to every institutional system clashes with the requirements of everyday living; that maybe in itself is the Babylon that will cause the collapse of humanity.

The complexities of intermingling sovereignty are shown by the lengthy legal pursuits of freedom advocates such as Kim Dotcom and Julian Assange. Millions of dollars are funding these legal battles. Are they themselves puppets of the sinister evils that are yet to be revealed?

CHAPTER FIFTEEN

CONTEMPORARY PROPHETS

Commercial Prophets Are Spilling the Beans

Maybe George Washington saw this day coming when he said, "If freedom of speech is taken away, then dumb and silent we may be led, like sheep to the slaughter."

Geeks, techies, coders—years ago, they were considered misfits, but now they're rising in social status as they dominate the world with their crafts. Like always, you'll hear it from the prophets first. Cracks in walls of secrecy have recently been spilling the beans about the purposes of data gathering.

Maybe the cracks are conscious choices of those who felt overcome by their morals. Alternatively, the cracks might have been made by opportunist, brilliant, technology craftsmen who want to determine the future. Technology is an opportunists' empire; just ask Bill, Steve, Mark, Larry, and Sergey. They are modern icons whose rapid rise to global status has overtaken the fortunes of many bygone generations.

Great opportunity often lies in the midst of great risks, so we have to identify the risks but not from an individual position. Snowden, Dotcom, and Assange are facing unprecedented danger by spilling those beans and warning this generation of looming regulation and domination beginning with the removal of personal Internet freedom.

They're in a sense techno-prophets of doom who have peered into the nexus of evil and speak the truth about what they have seen. Are they dousing the fire with gasoline rather than warning a foolish generation?

Do they further build exactly what they resist? Do they hinder or help the process of data mining?

Most likely, Snowden signed a contract of secrecy with the NSA, but now, he's breaking that contract to reveal things that troubled him morally. Is he a voice to help market the cause or a Judas in a great plot of betrayal?

In moral terms, Snow, Dotcom, and Assange are not preaching the gospel; rather, they're prophets of their own empires and warning their world of the coming system of control. Yet through their leaks, they're also preparing the world, normalizing the reality, so that when it comes, it will be embraced as necessary.

Have modern leakers such as Wikileaks taken over from where the 666 phobia left off in the previous decade? Certain prophecies have passed their expiration dates; the Jesus movement expected the year 2000 as the final days. Unlike twentieth-century end-times movements, Snow, Dotcom, and Assan, while far from being contemporaries of Shadrach, Meshach, and Abednego, are warning us of the growing plans for global control. But like the three in the burning flames, they are preaching from their isolation in their refusal to worship the idol of mega data controlled by Babylon the Great.

What they preach is the decoding of encrypted text, the very nexus of world control. Yet the message that is being preached is also encrypted. Well, did the prophet say, "Who has believed our report?"?

Revelation itself was encrypted; over 50 percent of human minds today could have had their beliefs of the future affected by this book. Although we call it "The Revelation of Jesus Christ," we never talk about that key word, that monster of inequality that starts the ball rolling, *apokalupsis*. The apocalypse of end-time calamities is realized from this book, which is also called the apocalypse. But the word *apocalypse* in Greek means "to take the cover off," not a global catastrophe.

Encryption and disclosure have a lot in common. To encrypt a message is in a sense to put a cover on it; to decode a message is in a sense to take the cover off and make known its contents. Every business has information that is personal to how it operates; it doesn't disclose it. In fact, it will frequently make people it employs sign nondisclosure agreements.

Revelation is the disclosure of Jesus Christ, but it contains many mysteries; it was written by the Master of mysteries, wisdom, knowledge, and foresight. A decoded Revelation gives us a full understanding of the Beast and what is about to happen. Yes, we now have the keys to decode the Beast.

Sovereign Authority

This system, the Beast of Babylon, will rule the governments of the world: "Authority was given him over every tribe, tongue, and nation" (Revelation 13:7 NKJV) and "He causes all, both small and great, rich and poor, free and slave, to receive a mark" (Revelation 13:16–17 NKJV).

How could any government, authority, or system achieve total control?' Would this be possible? Are the rich above the law? The poor and the middle class fought wars for freedom while the rich stayed far from the battlefields. You don't need to be a rocket scientist to understand some basic principles of how the governments and nations stay functional during the good and bad times; they rely on the rich.

Commerce was behind the scene in every war producing weapons, machines, clothes, and food. These were supplied by factories, farmers, and industry that were owned or controlled by rich people, as were the banks that funded the wars. All governments involved in war secured reliable companies and rich people to ensure their long-term survival.

During terrible times, businesspeople signed contracts and profited by them. While not all survived, new industries were formed and companies such as IBM and Boeing and the Swiss banks came out of World War II in strong positions.

If war makes an elite group of individuals prosper, how can those people be controlled? The declarations from Revelation about "He causes all" and "Authority over every" come to play here. Even just a few years ago, this could have appeared absolutely impossible, but then the techno-prophets revealed this.

Snow Quotes

#5 "The NSA has built an infrastructure that allows it to intercept almost everything." (27 Edward Snowden Quotes About U.S. Government Spying That Should Send A Chill Up Your Spine
By Michael Snyder, on June 10ᵗʰ, 2013)

#6 "With this capability, the vast majority of human communications are automatically ingested without targeting. If I wanted to see your e-mails or your wife's phone, all I have to do is use intercepts. I can get your e-mails, passwords, phone records, credit cards." (27 Edward Snowden Quotes About U.S. Government Spying That Should Send A Chill Up Your Spine

By Michael Snyder, on June 10th, 2013)

#7 "Any analyst at any time can target anyone. Any selector, anywhere ... I, sitting at my desk, certainly had the authorities to wiretap anyone, from you or your accountant, to a federal judge, to even the President." (27 Edward Snowden Quotes About U.S. Government Spying That Should Send A Chill Up Your Spine

By Michael Snyder, on June 10th, 2013)

#10 "They are intent on making every conversation and every form of behavior in the world known to them." (27 Edward Snowden Quotes About U.S. Government Spying That Should Send A Chill Up Your Spine

By Michael Snyder, on June 10th, 2013_

Global electronic transmissions are in some way routed through the United States, which harvests that data and retrieves it as it pleases. As you can see in the seventh quote, NSA has the power to collect data from anyone, including a federal judge or a president and even people abroad; this system has no prejudices; it encompasses everything and everyone. Even the rich and their complicated finances can be caught in this web. This is an incredible prediction. While it is not the end to Revelation 13, it's certainly heading in that direction. Snowden is warning the earth of pending dangers. Can we avert the fulfillment of Revelation?

From Revelation 13, in which the beginning days of this system are revealed, it continues to the full revealing of this Beast of Babylon, a huge monster ruling this earth. It's controlling all the commerce, even that involving human bodies and souls.

""The kings of the earth who committed fornication and
lived luxuriously with her will weep and lament for her,

when they see the smoke of her burning, "standing at a distance for fear of her torment, saying, 'Alas, alas, that great city Babylon, that mighty city! For in one hour your judgment has come.'"And the merchants of the earth will weep and mourn over her, for no one buys their merchandise anymore: "merchandise of gold and silver, precious stones and pearls, fine linen and purple, silk and scarlet, every kind of citron wood, every kind of object of ivory, every kind of object of most precious wood, bronze, iron, and marble; "and cinnamon and incense, fragrant oil and frankincense, wine and oil, fine flour and wheat, cattle and sheep, horses and chariots, and bodies and souls of men. "The fruit that your soul longed for has gone from you, and all the things which are rich and splendid have gone from you, and you shall find them no more at all. "The merchants of these things, who became rich by her, will stand at a distance for fear of her torment, weeping and wailing, "and saying, 'Alas, alas, that great city that was clothed in fine linen, purple, and scarlet, and adorned with gold and precious stones and pearls! 'For in one hour such great riches came to nothing.' Every shipmaster, all who travel by ship, sailors, and as many as trade on the sea, stood at a distance. (Revelation 18:9–17 NKJV).

CHAPTER SIXTEEN

A FINAL TRIBUTE

Escaping the Silent World

We live in a world that often prefers to remain silent rather than raise questions about issues. There are many with silent convictions skipping through life as silent witnesses. Don't ask, and they won't tell; ask, and they'll still not tell. Theirs is a fragile spiritual existence in need of a deeper reality. They are alive but dormant. They are hidden by the modernist world with a silent view; they are choked by the cunning master of unseen games who reigns in the unseen and silent kingdom of earth.

Who would talk when the gag order is made? Who would whisper when the threat is against social sanity? Thoughts, impressions, and unseen thinking rages in the dark, unseen seat of the mind. As skies that weigh on seas, unseen matters weigh on human consciousness. We talk about what we know and proudly display our knowledge; who will voice matters of indeterminable thoughts?

Subtle people refuse to admit anything; they shake their heads and say, "No, not me." The interrogator looks sternly, wanting to shed light on the matter. How can one determine what is true and what isn't? Anyone can say anything in a dark room; it's "reality TV" dressed in a believable fashion.

Is our consciousness too beggarly to accept any other than what is considered acceptable? Real or virtual? It's no longer important what people think they are; it's what they want you to think they are that's paramount. If a person were to say about others, "They believe, they practice religion, they're Christian, and they go to church," who could say otherwise? "Well, good on them" would be a good reply. Yet a statement about their faith is not a statement of faith. It's a possible glimpse of conviction, but it could be a deception. Faith is determined by what is truly coming out of the mouth.

The heart believes, but salvation is achieved by the confession of faith through the mouth. To speak the words of your belief, to proclaim that which you believe will justify you if it's the truth or condemn you if it's false.

What is unseen is made evident, justified by faith. What remains hidden is not evident; if it remains hidden, who can be sure of the outcome? Maybe you'll find glory, and maybe you won't. God will be your judge, but you'll know what the outcome is only after it's too late to change.

When your person leaves your body, you'll be seen according to the life you led. All things will be exposed to the light. Blindness will no longer have a hold on the mind. Does the darkness own you? Or does the light own you? Will you gamble your life based on things you have no control over? Will you play with darkness and hide from the light? Will you take that chance, which is reserved for that day?

Only in the earthly realm do you have control. When your body falls to the ground, when it takes its final breath and your person is no longer held, you will lose control of the earthly realm and it will lose control of you. You have charge of your affairs on earth; you are subject to earth's jurisdiction. The law, governments, and everything produced is for the order and pleasure of the earthly body.

When the body permanently fails, all law and order relating to that unique earth body also pass away. Property is divided among the living, not the dead. All penalties of wrong and all rewards of right done by someone is no more. No longer does that one have authority on earth; no longer can that one make decisions that affect the living. They no longer go to meetings, drive cars, or have a social life.

Those who depart earth cannot avoid the spiritual realities they are subject to. All earthly fantasies will be measured by the real, the spiritual. Will Muslims find paradise? Will Hindu find new, earthly bodies? Will agnostics find knowledge? Will atheists find nothing? Will Christians find salvation?

In the ultimate reality, no myth is relevant. The dead have no place among the living. The world of the departed is hidden from us; make sure what you hope for is more than just a hope or a toss of the dice. No matter what Hinduism says, we will die just once. What happens then?

Those who think we have more than one shot at dying better find some good proof of that so they're not just gambling on the idea. If you have even the smallest of impressions that this God in Jesus Christ thing is real, why would you ever chance it on a gamble?

Today we live and tomorrow we die. We will have no more power to change anything if we've played our cards wrong. The cake is done. The clay is out of the kiln. The fruit is plucked from the tree. It is complete. It can't be changed. Did the pot last through the firing? It's too late to change the form. Was the fruit an orange? It's too late to change the seed. Was the cake tasty? It's too late to change the ingredients.

On earth, we can change things when they or we go wrong; we just rework the program and change the outcome. When we die, we can't go back and change anything. Millions of people make wrong decisions every day, but they can change them. The dead can't.

In death, the unknown will be known. Will you pass go? Will you pass through the gate or refused entry? What determines this end? What can change your future from an uncertainty to a certainty? A conviction is only a conviction as long as it's left in darkness. Nothing is justified in the heart or in the mind without words. Words need to correspond.

With the heart, you believe in righteousness; with the mouth, you confess and gain salvation. You want the assurance millions have discovered through the ages. You want joy and happiness, to know everything will be okay. You want the peace that keeps you through all the days and even at the gates of death. You cannot just parrot others' words or the creed of an organization; you have to personally confess to them and believe them. That is the true meaning of coming to the light.

There is salvation through no other name than that of Jesus Christ. Eternal life can be found only through Jesus, whom God sent to give us hope and save us. He will give you the peace that surpasses all understanding. It's no scam; you don't need to donate money. It's free. To make your salvation sure, to make your future certain, say so with your mouth.

It's not a case of saying simply, "Oh well, I confessed these things as a child, so yes, I do believe." That might not stand. The words you speak today will determine your tomorrow. Why take the chance? Why gamble on your childhood words? Only the now can save you. Here are the words you should speak to save yourself.

"Jesus, Son of God, I believe you were sent by God the Father of heaven and earth. Jesus, you were born of a virgin, you were given an earthly body, and you died for my sins and my shortfalls. I couldn't be saved, but Jesus, you came and saved me. I repent of all my sins and unbelief and believe in God and Jesus Christ, the only true Son of God. I receive now all your plan of salvation right now in the name of Jesus. I confess John 3:16: 'For God so loved the world that He gave His only begotten Son, that whoever believes in Him should not perish but have everlasting life.'

"I'm believing in you right now, Jesus, I'm believing right now that the true God has saved me through you. I'm saved and forgiven by the blood of Jesus Christ spilled on the cross. Lord, you have saved me from hell and promised me heaven. I give you my life and ask you, dear Lord, to give me the assurance you promised and the peace that surpasses all understanding. Please lead me; I will follow you. I confess and pray this in the name of Jesus."

About the Author

Many people are disturbed by these troubled times, Graeme brings a fresh understanding as to what God is doing in these days.

Ordained in Tulsa in 1998, Graeme has a passion for life and God. Married for 30 years with five children, a busnessman and lay preacher. His passion to understand the relevance and God's word, into todays world, has been the driving force of his writing.

Now he writes from a body of work, collected for over thirty years. As well as a deep and long career in our modern technology age, spanning from his early days as an electronics technician.

Printed in the United States
By Bookmasters